*Vision for the
Local Congregation:*

GOD'S PEOPLE ON MISSION THROUGH MINISTRY

VISION FOR THE LOCAL CONGREGATION

GOD'S PEOPLE ON MISSION THROUGH MINISTRY

by

Gerald G. Nevitt

Published by

The Church of God in Michigan
Service Center
4212 Alpha Street
Lansing, Michigan 48910

Vision for the Local Congregation: God's People On Mission Through Ministry

Vision and strategy are essential to the realization of God's purpose for the local congregation. Dr. Gerald Nevitt has guided congregations in a variety of cultural settings in the discovery of a vision and implementation of strategies. He has been an effective, disciplined pastor. He has led the Michigan Church of God in a creative program for evangelism and discipleship, providing entry points and participation levels for congregations of every size. He has served on national task forces that were asked to discern the present situation and the opportunity for the Church of God (Anderson, Indiana) in the 21st century. Gerald knows what he is talking about when he writes about visioning! Visioning is the fundamental strategy for Kingdom work!

Pastors and lay leaders will find the chapter on "Developing a Mission Strategy" particularly helpful. Obstacles to mission and ministry are thoughtfully identified in another chapter. Christians who are serious about the Great Commission will appreciate this biblically based, practical manual prepared by a leader with a heart for the ministry of the local church. It is my hope that Dr. Nevitt will have opportunity to share his studies and insights with several groups throughout the United States.

— **Dr. Oral Withrow**
Church Growth Ministries
Board of Church Extension
and Home Missions of the
Church of God
Anderson, Indiana

Copyright © 1995
Dr. Gerald G. Nevitt
All rights reserved
ISBN 1-887998-01-2

Typography by
Graphic Services Company
307 Colfax Avenue
Benton Harbor, Michigan 49022

Printed by
Patterson Printing
1550 Territorial Road
Benton Harbor, Michigan 49022

TABLE OF CONTENTS

INTRODUCTION vii
REFOCUS THE VISION

CHAPTER ONE 1
A PERSONAL JOURNEY

CHAPTER TWO 11
THEOLOGICAL FOUNDATIONS FOR
MISSION AND MINISTRY

CHAPTER THREE 29
THE VISION THEME:
GOD'S PEOPLE ON MISSION THROUGH
MINISTRY

CHAPTER FOUR 39
WHAT IS YOUR VISION?

CHAPTER FIVE 47
DEVELOPING A MISSION STRATEGY
    MISSION PURPOSE 47
    MISSION CONTEXT 51
      Know Your Community
      Congregational History
      Present Ministry and Worker Analysis
    MISSION STATEMENT 56
    MISSION PLANNING 58
      Mission Goal Setting
      Implementation
      Evaluation

iv *Vision for the Local Congregation:*
   God's People on Mission Through Ministry

CHAPTER SIX 65
**WHEN FELLOWSHIP AND
MISSION COLLIDE**

CHAPTER SEVEN 75
IDENTIFYING THE OBSTACLES
   SIN AND DISOBEDIENCE 76
   SHALLOW FAITH AND LOSS OF VISION . 78
   THE SINGLE CELL 82
   COMMON STRUCTURAL BARRIERS 84
   DESTRUCTIVE CONFLICT 87

CHAPTER EIGHT 91
**AFFIRMING LEADERSHIP FOR THE
MISSION OF THE CONGREGATION**
   THE POWER OF BLESSING 92
   PASTORAL ADVISORY TEAM 96
   NETWORKING AND MENTORING 99
   LEADERSHIP AND MISSION 101
   LEADERSHIP AND STYLE 104

CHAPTER NINE	113
HOW TO MOBILIZE A CONGREGATION FOR MINISTRY	
SPIRITUAL GIFTS THEOLOGY	115
STEPS FOR IMPLEMENTING SPIRITUAL GIFTS	117
Discern	
Discover	
Dedicate	
Deploy	
Develop	
CONTEMPORARY MODELS	123
Informal and Unstructured Model	
Spiritual Gifts Advisor Model	
Willow Creek Model	
Skyline Model	
Bear Valley Model	
LEADERSHIP FOR MINISTRY	128
The Spiritual Leadership Component	
The Practical Leadership Component	
The Relational Leadership Component	
CHAPTER TEN	137
COPING WITH CHANGE	
CHANGE: PROBLEM AND POSSIBILITY	138
RECEPTIVITY TO CHANGE	142
THE CHANGE PROCESS	148
STRATEGIES FOR CHANGE	150
CHANGE AND CONFLICT	153
THE SPIRITUAL DIMENSION	156

CHAPTER ELEVEN 159
A PLAN FOR RENEWAL AND VISION
STEP ONE -
 PERSONAL COMMITMENT 160
STEP TWO -
 PURSUE GOD'S VISION FOR
 MISSION AND MINISTRY
 IN THE LOCAL CONGREGATION 162
STEP THREE -
 MOBILIZE FOR CONTINUING
 EFFECTIVENESS:
 GOAL SETTING AND PLANNING 166
STEP FOUR -
 AGREE ON THE MEANS OF MINISTRY . 169

CHAPTER TWELVE 177
ANTICIPATING THE HARVEST
PRAYER 179
VISION 182
FAITH 184
OBEDIENCE 185
INCREASING THE ANTICIPATION FOR
 THE HARVEST 187
LEADERSHIP FOR THE TASK 188
PARTNERSHIP IN MISSION AND
 MINISTRY 190

SOURCES CONSULTED 193

LIST OF ILLUSTRATIONS
Figure 1. ...... Mission Strategy Cycle 59
Figure 2. . Concern for People and Task Grid ... 71
Figure 3. ...... Berry Bucket Theory 145
Figure 4. .... Level of Discontent 148
Figure 5. .... Harvest Circle 187

REFOCUS THE VISION

God has a vision for our generation. And if we Christians are to accomplish this vision, we must understand it. What is God's purpose of local congregations? What is his grand design?

Can we discover in the biblical account a plan that would help us, first, to comprehend and, second, to do his will? Before we can be effective in mission and ministry, we — as part of the local congregation — must have a clear picture of the intention of God for us.

I believe God is giving many pastors and leaders a renewed vision of what he wants the local church to be and do in the coming years. I admit to a sense of spiritual renewal in my relationship with God as I have talked and prayed with persons concerned about the church. My spirit and my thinking have been energized by the moving of God in many congregations. I believe the decade of the 1990's can be an unprecedented period of renewal and growth for the church — and here's the catch — if local congregations embrace God's vision.

We live in an historic time. Recent events have been extraordinary. From the crumbling of the Berlin wall to the collapse of Communism, there is new opportunty. People hunger for the Good News.

We are reminded that the New Testament uses the word <u>chronos</u> to speak of the succession of events within history. However, the word <u>kairos</u> designates the never-to-be-repeated "historic" incidents that have eternal significance in God's plan. We now live in God's <u>kairos</u> for the proclamation and the incarnation of the gospel in this generation. It is an opportunity for everyone committed to the Great Commission to embrace a new vision of what God is calling his people to be and do. The local congregation can capture God's vision and allow it to guide the church's work into the next century.

VISION FOR MISSION AND MINISTRY

Sometime ago, a pastor friend asked me, "What is your vision for the church?" As I stumbled through several ideas and concepts that were important for me just then, I realized my vision for the church was dim and distant. I was operating on some deep convictions which had guided me in the past, but I did not have a clear and current vision for my personal ministry and for the church. Indeed, I had not sufficiently struggled in prayer to discover the nature of God's vision for his church.

Shortly afterward, a local congregation invited me to share my vision for the church. Out of these challenges I began thinking and praying for insight into God's vision and plan for the church. In the midst of this personal quest, God began to form in my mind and heart a sharper, more distinct picture of his intention for the church. This vision for the church can be summarized in a statement which has taken on increased meaning for me: The church is to be God's people on mission through ministry.

THREE AIMS FOR GOD'S PEOPLE ON MISSION THROUGH MINISTRY.

God's purpose for the church gives direction for the activity of the local congregation. These aims define the focus for the church's program.

1. To be uniquely the people of God.

A vision for the church begins with what God desires for a people who are uniquely his own. The church is comprised of people who are "after the heart of God," (Jeremiah 3:15). This speaks of the relationship we have with our Lord and what he is helping us to become. We are to be a people who are alive in faith and vital in our connection with a living Lord. He is the center of our experience together. As a people, we are to seek, worship and praise him with a freshness that attracts the unconverted and uncommitted. The church is to thrive and grow through the genuine quality of life in Christ that we share. By who we are and what he is making us to be, we are God's representatives to live out the message of healing and wholeness in a broken world. Yes, we are chosen by God, but we are chosen for service and ministry, not for special privilege.

2. *To be on mission for God.*

Our purpose is to achieve God's mission in the world. God does not call us to be an ingrown, self-absorbed mutual admiration society. His call is to accomplish the mission task, the redeeming activity of God. We are to complete the mission of Christ on this earth. We are called to be a "light to the nations" (Isaiah 42:6). That global responsibility begins with every community and extends to every state and nation. Indeed, the church does not exist for its own comfort and well-being. The church exists to share the message of love and redemption with all persons. Its reason for being? To serve as a beacon for those who have not heard or responded to the call of God to salvation. The central motivation for the church is to be on God's mission to bring all men and women into a right relationship with him. The church is to be the embodiment of reconciliation in our society.

3. *To be serving persons with the ministry of Christ.*

The focus of the activity and life within the body of believers is ministry to persons. The church is the hands of our Lord touching the lives of people where there is estrangement and hurt. The first priority is to share the "good news" of hope in Christ. This is often expressed in compassionate ministries which lift and affirm people to be children of a loving and just God. The church is to meet people at their point of need and not on the basis of our tradition or churchly expectations. Centering the life of the church on ministry means that the church will take leadership responsibility for healing the ills and injustices of our society. Our intent is to be representatives of Christ to influence our culture with his ways and his spirit.

With this understanding as our guide, God is calling his church to a new level of intensity as we seek to be "God's People on Mission through Ministry." When the year 2000 A.D. dawns, will we be able to look back upon this decade as the time when we responded wholeheartedly to the call of God to be uniquely his people engaged authentically in his mission and ministry?

CHAPTER ONE
A PERSONAL JOURNEY

Leaders responsible to guide the mission and ministry of the church must systematically think through the implications of the congregation's life and activity in the light of God's Word. God's will and vision for the church are contained in his Word. However, our theology of mission and ministry may be based in the Bible, often arises from our experience. That is, we formulate theology in the context of personal and congregational life by doing ministry. With the current emphasis on the personal and practical, I want to share something of my spiritual journey. It is my story and it has led me to my convictions about the present need for renewal in the church.

My concern for vital local congregations has grown out of my lifelong involvement with the Church of God movement. From birth, I have been nurtured and prepared, spiritually and vocationally, for ministry. My parents were converted early in their marriage and came to see the Church of God as the fulfillment of God's plan to reveal his truth regarding the unity and holiness of his people.

Although conservative in lifestyle and evangelical in biblical interpretation, this fresh truth about the church gave cohesion and substance to the life of the movement and the local congregation. My friend and mentor, Gale Hetrick, describes the early leaders of this reformation movement as possessing a motivating factor.

> *They were a people who had discovered "a secret" which they called "the truth" or "this truth." "The truth" had to do with their vision of the church. The church, they said, was composed of those who were in Christ, the saved, the redeemed, the forgiven, the holy. They saw the church as an end in itself. They insisted that it stood alone without*

Vision for the Local Congregation:
God's People on Mission Through Ministry

creed, hierarchy, or buildings, and that all who were in the church were members one of another, to stand unsullied by the powers of hell.[1]

As a young person, I became immersed in the life of a local congregation of the Church of God in Indianapolis, Indiana. It was the center for my social and spiritual life. I saw the congregational activities and events that filled the calendar and shaped those years as full of meaning and personal satisfaction. The church provided the wonderful ingredients of childhood: buddies with whom to run and laugh, girls to tease and torment, outings to excite and entice. Benefiting from the special attention and care of parents, pastors and teachers who modeled the Christian way, I easily committed my life to Jesus.

My experiences in the local church as a teenager served only to reinforce the direction of my life. A mixed quartet developed from the youth group, and we sang in special meetings and youth events. Church music in the church became a first love and an expression of personal development which provided many opportunities for ministry as time went along. In the course of these activities, I was challenged by a young neighbor pastor to consider Christian ministry even though I was on a track for electrical engineering and quite happy with that course. My first preaching experience was in an open-air tent revival meeting held on a vacant lot.

The only negative memories that I have of my early church fellowship came out of conflict situations which caused people to leave that local church. Even though I did not understand the issues, I knew that something was wrong. Certain leaders were quite unhappy with other leaders. These were people that I cared for and loved very much. Yet, the conflict was evidently more than they could bear. Eventually, I, too, left that fellowship in disappointment and quite perplexed about the conduct of the leadership.

Although my commitment to ministry was genuine and positive, my confidence and self-perception were lacking. During my years at Anderson College, however, caring professors and teachers as well as tolerant leaders in local congregations reassured me that one day all would come together and I would make a contribution to the work of God. After my sophomore year, I married a beautiful girl who had hoped to marry a missionary. JoRene and I took on the responsibility of family life. Then came two hard years of trying to balance a forty-hour work week, full-time college studies and home life that was complicated by my wife who loved to travel and sing with a vocal trio as she had in her single days.

Graduation relieved some of the pressure. But I immediately accepted a position with the East Side Church of God in Anderson, Indiana, as a minister of music and youth — and janitor. The reality is that the invitation came on the strength of my wife's personality and singing ability. I was learning humility. However, I lost the janitor portion of the job after one year because my priorities were in the wrong place (so they said).

With this inauspicious start, I served as an associate minister in Anderson for more than two years and then four years in New Albany, Indiana. Our two sons were born during this time and I continued my seminary work on a part-time basis at the Anderson School of Theology and the Southern Baptist Seminary in Louisville, Kentucky.

My pastoral ministry in local congregations covered nineteen years in three states: Illinois, Michigan and California. While not precisely a church planter, I was the founding pastor of a new project church in Champaign, Illinois. It was hard, exhilarating, often disappointing work; yet these were some of the best years of ministry for me. This church fellowship grew from four families to a strong multiracial congregation with a very functional multiple-purpose facility in a thriving college community. I believe God was pleased with the ministry of this fledgling congregation.

The next twelve years were very important for my ministry and for my family. Otsego, a small community in southwest Michigan, became the place where I hammered out ministry concepts and relational skills with God, my family and the local congregation. It was a learning experience for the congregation and for me! I came to them as a brash, determined but somewhat insecure thirty-three year old minister who had not much patience with "the way things have been done." As a music director and new church pastor, I had been accustomed to "conducting" and being in charge of the "score." The first five years were not harmonious.

Yet, they tolerated me and loved my family. I grew in my ministry skills and in my deep affection for the church people. God blessed the congregation with modest growth, effective youth ministry (two handsome sons didn't detract at all), excellent worship, new educational facilities, enriched stature in the community, and a consciousness of shared ministry.

During this period I became very active in cooperative ministry with the Church of God in Michigan. After directing a youth camp for several years, I took on the responsibility of coordinating seven youth camps and planning for back packing and canoe trips. Serving on the Division of Christian Education, I worked with others to set up the new Division of Youth Ministries for the Church of God in Michigan. When my oldest son's life was transformed as the result of a bicycle ministry sponsored by Anderson College, I prodded Gale Hetrick until we purchased the used "chuck wagon" and twenty lightweight ten-speed bikes. The hours and hours of hard labor on that ministry by the Otsego people and my family were not wasted. "Wheelin' Free in the Son," as it was named, was an evangelistic tool instrumental in shaping the lives of many young people across Michigan and Indiana.

In June 1981, with our sons graduated from high school, JoRene and I responded to a call to serve a local congregation of the Church of God in Pomona, California. This was a whirlwind episode which I have since referred to as my "Egypt experience." I became what Lyle Schaller, a nationally known church consultant, has called "an unintended interim" pastor. And the church was in an obvious decline. The previous pastor was a popular, nationally recognized charismatic preacher. Nothing I tried there clicked. I was unhappy, and the congregation did not seem thrilled with me. Although these were fine, dedicated people, God was teaching me the realities of urban ministry. I came very, very close to bailing out and finding another vocation. Fortunately, God had other plans and the General Assembly leaders in Michigan called me to return as the Executive Secretary of the Church of God in Michigan. Although this was a marvelous opportunity, I struggled with the decision because I was a pastor at heart, and I still had unfulfilled dreams for the congregation in Pomona.

Although my present chapter of my ministry is still too fresh for me to be objective as to its full meaning and significance, I have found a real purpose for ministry. My gifts are sharpened by the demands and expectations of pastors and leaders for the congregations of the Church of God in Michigan. Discerning God's will and catching his vision for the church are primary responsibilities for me. Working with pastors and leaders in existing congregations and establishing a climate for planting new congregations are the context. The goal is the growth of God's kingdom! My share and contribution in this section of the vineyard is to facilitate and develop the structure which supports and energizes leaders in the harvest.

As I look back at almost seven years as an associate minister and nineteen years as a pastor, I am now aware of the frustration that I kept under control. Engaged in preaching and teaching, week after week, month after month, I was

6 Vision for the Local Congregation: God's People on Mission Through Ministry

bothered by my inability to reach people outside of the church who desperately needed to hear the Good News of God's love and forgiveness. Even though my intention was to go into my community with the gospel, I was consumed with the task of keeping oil on the wheels of church machinery. I was an ecclesiastical engineer! I was unable to spend much time or energy directly or intentionally in the evangelistic task except for my pulpit ministry.

Indeed, early in my ministry I was working under the assumption that everything I or the church did was evangelistic. My spiritual pilgrimage has led me from a broader more inclusive view that all church life is redemptive to a much more focused view of the task of the church. While the local congregation is called to do many activities that are good and essential, I now believe that mission and evangelism must be the central task of the church.

My current exposure to congregational church life and to cooperative work in Michigan leads me to a conclusion. The most important task before us today is to forge out of our life together a commitment to the mission of Jesus Christ. He came to "seek and save" (Luke 19:10) the lost. The purpose of the church is to glorify God. The first priority is to make disciples.

In too many places, congregations are dying for lack of spiritual life and commitment to the mission and purpose of God's redemptive plan. Sometimes the only energy generated comes from conflict situations where the leaders vie for control or fuss over insignificant issues. In other circumstances, the problems are the honest struggle of leaders to discern and implement God's direction for their mission and ministry. Several events may underscore the severity of the problem.

When I took the responsibility as Executive Secretary of the Church of God in Michigan in January 1984, within the first six weeks I faced six new full-blown conflict situations in local churches. One congregation was divided by the immoral behavior of the pastor. In another, the leaders were fighting among themselves over the leadership style of the pastor. The very life of these congregations was threatened. Any idealism that I had regarding my responsibility quickly faded. Someone jokingly remarked that if my success continued at this pace the Church of God in Michigan might be reduced to almost zero congregations after ten years. However, the effect of this onslaught caused me to seek and develop a system that addressed conflict before it became public. Certainly, conflict is a continuing and agonizing problem, but I have been forced to be proactive in dealing with it.

During this time, four new congregations were established in the aftermath of conflict. No one can ever calculate the personal pain encountered by the pastors, leaders and congregations that endured such situations. Although I do not have Solomon's wisdom, I have tried to stand with individuals and congregations in conflict. I have felt compassion and genuine caring for all the persons involved. Sadly, I have not always been perceived by participants in this manner. I pray daily for discernment and God's guidance.

Without apology, I have become aggressive in dealing with conflict, even when not called upon. I am determined to confront people as early in the process as possible and work with our Department of Ministry to bring about reconciliation. My goal is the increase of the kingdom of God in spite of the difficulty. Interestingly enough, leaders in three of these instances made a conscious effort to separate amicably and to birth a new congregation without hostility. For the most part, while the pain of conflict remains, the congregations have produced modest growth and are now productive, healthy, ministering congregations.

Concurrent with these developments, the Division of Church Extension for the Church of God in Michigan began to move away from its traditional stance of providing subsistence money to keep congregations alive. When little prospect for a viable congregation existed because of ineffective leadership or poor track record of accountability, these problems were faced realistically. The Division began to provide training opportunities for leaders and entered into "Partnership in Ministry Agreements" with congregations. These formal covenants between the Division and the local church provided for mutual support and accountability. While all of this had been attempted with varying degrees of success in the past, a new mood of intentionality was apparent. The direction is now to be proactive in assisting congregations with growth and outreach. It was an effort to go beyond the maintenance of church life to effective mission and ministry.

All of this had a tremendous impact upon me personally. I was becoming more and more convinced that congregations engaging in "business as usual" were doomed to experience decline and ineffective ministry. My training in the principles of church growth compounded my personal dilemma and made my ministry seem like only a holding action. After all, the office out of which I was working was called the "Service Center." By definition, I was in the maintenance business.

Without realizing it, I was working myself into a corner. Through my colleagues in the Service Center and the efforts of many dedicated pastors and lay leaders, we were making a difference in the life and ministry of the church across Michigan. Our cooperative ministry was growing and becoming more demanding and time consuming for everyone involved, not just for me. Yet, I could not let up or appear to be overwhelmed by the immensity of "the pressure of my concern for all the churches" (2 Corinthians 11:28).

I write this account only to detail the personal renewal that God has initiated in my own life. I believe that it is through personal renewal that congregations — even state and national organizations — can be redirected and inspired to a fresh vision of what God wants to achieve in and through his church.

In the spring of 1990, I had reached a maximum saturation level in my personal ministry to pastors and congregations. I was spending more time on the road to and from assignments than I was spending in direct involvement with leaders and congregations, or so I thought. I was road weary and emotionally drained with little reserve capacity for taking some of the hits that often come with the natural responsibility and expectations of people for the office. I felt I was ineffective and brittle. Indeed, I concluded that I could not drive any more miles, meet with any more committees, initiate any more conflict resolution strategies, be the encourager for any more pastors and leaders than what I was presently doing. Working harder was not going to reduce the number of unfulfilled aspirations that I had and others had for the church in Michigan. Frankly, I had all I could do, all I could take! Something had to change. My devotional life was very poor. I was not much fun to be with and the joy was gone. I felt neither God nor my wife could take much pleasure in my company.

On a trip home from Anderson, Indiana, to Lansing on what has become for me the most boring stretch of highway in the United States, God intervened with a spiritual insight which started me on a path to personal renewal. I was listening to the tapes of a recent ministries conference to fill the time void and break the monotony of the drive. The speaker was dealing with the issue of personal prayer life. I was affected from the very beginning of the tape. He then used a verse of scripture through which God spoke to me unmistakably. "Then will I give you shepherds after my own heart who will lead you with knowledge and understanding" (Jeremiah 3:15).

That moving vehicle became a place of retreat and renewal. In those moments, I regained a personal presence with the living Lord and a new perspective on my ministry and service to the church. Although later study of the verse would confirm the insights of this time with God, I knew that "doing" ministry was not my problem. Being "after the heart" of God was the issue. My relationship with God — who I was to "be" in his eyes — was far more significant than what I could accomplish for him. Spiritually, I was on a new and exciting path.

Coupled with this experience was the challenge of my colleagues for a new vision for the Church of God in Michigan. That pressure and the fact that I had, by any estimate, only twelve years before retirement to make a difference in the life of the church through my leadership caused me to do some soul searching. What did God want me to be and what did he want me to do? What lasting contribution would I be able to make? While these questions were personal and introspective, they were not overwhelming and burdensome. I had found a new freedom and confidence in my quest. My real task was to be close to God. He would supply the leaders who were "after my own heart" who would lead "with knowledge and understanding."

I learned two very valuable spiritual principles. The first was that "being" is a greater priority than "doing." God's work must be done and it is the most important task in the world. However, it is his mission and ministry, not ours. We must be "connected to the vine" to be a fruitful branch.

The second principle set the agenda for my ministry. The "shepherds," better translated "leaders," who seek the heart and mind of God were to be the focus of my efforts. Assisting in the development and empowerment of leadership for the mission and ministry of the Kingdom of God was the call that God had placed on my life.

ENDNOTES

[1] Gale Hetrick, LAUGHTER AMONG THE TRUMPETS (Lansing, Michigan: The Church of God in Michigan, 1980), VII.

CHAPTER TWO
THEOLOGICAL FOUNDATIONS FOR MISSION AND MINISTRY

Even a brief overview of a theology for the church's mission and ministry cannot be reduced to a statement or a popularized slogan. But from the pages of the biblical record we can distill the truth which will give us the wisdom to know his will and guide our activity. While the Bible is our primary source, we will also remain open to the lessons learned from the experience of dedicated men and women engaged in mission and ministry. Nine statements are affirmations for understanding the core of the local congregation's mission and ministry.

1. *The Redeeming Activity of God is the Basis for Mission and Ministry.*

The superstructure of the mission and ministry assignment lies on the foundation of the saving and redeeming activity of God in history. Indeed, the scripture that is very near to the heart of the matter declares, "God so loved the world that he gave his one and only Son...," (John 3:16). God has loved his creation from the beginning and has sought to establish a covenant of love and mutual trust between himself and humankind. The advent of the Savior, Jesus, was the culmination of the saving activity of God. It was the pinnacle of what he had been doing throughout the course of human history.

The Bible itself tells the story of humankind's willful rejection of God's plan. By choosing the way of sinful rebellion, humankind fell from a unique relationship with the Creator. Yet, as recorded in the events of Israel, God continued to make himself known in extraordinary historical occurrences. His intent was to show his love and impart to men and women a knowledge of Yahweh who sought to bring them back into fellowship with himself.

The story of the Bible and of history itself is the history of God as he calls humankind back to himself. It is "salvation history" and the record of God who directed events within history to restore humankind by his loving kindness and gracious acts toward them.[2]

The saga of Israel is the story of all peoples. The Apostle Paul declares that "all have sinned and fall short of the glory of God...," (Romans 3:23). Yet, God continued to reach out to his creation to seek a way to redeem and bring persons to wholeness and oneness with himself. As the writer of Hebrews explains, "In the past God spoke to our forefathers through the prophets at many times and various ways, but in these last days he has spoken to us by his Son...," (Hebrews 1:1,2).

The foundation of the church's mission and ministry rests on the fact that Jesus was the full expression of God seeking to redeem humankind from enslavement to sin and despair. "For God was pleased to have all his fullness dwell in him, and through him to reconcile to himself all things, whether things on earth or in heaven, by making peace through his blood, shed on the cross" (Colossians 1:19,20).

The cornerstone of the church's mission and ministry is explained in the words of the apostle:

Therefore, if anyone is in Christ, he is a new creation; the old has gone, the new has come! All this is from God, who reconciled us to himself through Christ and gave us the ministry of reconciliation: that God was reconciling the world to himself in Christ, not counting men's sins against them (2 Corinthians 5:17 - 19a).

2. The Task of the Church Is to Convey the Good News of Salvation.

The church, then, becomes responsible to respond to that essential understanding of the saving act of God in the life, death and resurrection of Jesus. It becomes the task of the church to convey the gospel, the "good news" of Jesus and his saving and reconciling work, to a humanity that is lost and without hope.

The New Testament clearly urges the church to engage in this task. There is no question regarding the appropriateness of the task. The church has no alternative if it is to accept the mandate of scripture.

Jesus' words are plain: "...you will be my witnesses in Jerusalem, and in all Judea and Samaria, and to the ends of the earth" (Acts 1:8).

All authority in heaven and on earth has been given to me. Therefore go and make disciples of all nations, baptizing them in the name of the Father and of the Son and of the Holy Spirit, and teaching them to obey everything I have commanded you. And surely I will be with you always, to the very end of the age (Matthew 28:18-20).

When the Apostle Paul rejoiced in the reconciling work of God, he was very clear about who was to convey that message of truth to the world. "And he has committed to us the message of reconciliation. We are therefore Christ's ambassadors, as though God were making his appeal through us" (1 Corinthians 5:19b-20a).

Not only in the direct commands to the followers of Christ do we find the imperative to "go" and to convey the gospel, but we also discover that God has used "the people of God" in every generation to be bearers of the salvation story. The call of God and election of a "special people" is a theme of the Old Testament which identifies the means God uses to convey his love and redemption.[3] It is this motif which challenges the church to be the people of the new covenant.[4]

> *But you are a chosen people, a royal priesthood, a holy nation, a people belonging to God, that you may declare the praises of him who called you out of darkness into his wonderful light. Once you were not a people, but now you are the people of God;...* (1 Peter 2:9,10).

God has a special possession, a people whom he has called. This call is not to be thought of as a privilege and a place of honor. Rather, the choice of the new Israel, the church, as his people is for the purpose of extending the redeeming and saving activity of God to all people and nations.[5] Thus, the choosing of the "people of God" is so that they might be a "light for the nations" (Isaiah 42:6). "When the people of God are truly renewed they will become the servant of the Lord, embodying the new covenant, then the Lord will be able to fulfill his wider purposes through them."[6]

The means the church uses to convey the Good News is important because it is the expression of our belief about what God expects of us. In other words, we do not choose just any means to convey the gospel. The means, itself, is a declaration of what we believe to be true about the will of God for the church in its relationship to the world.

Three words have become powerful characterizations of the role and mission of the church. These are the words "proclaim," "represent," and "demonstrate." While the concept of proclamation cannot be confined to the mere verbal telling of the story of Jesus, it is rooted in the oral communication of the gospel. The New Testament words "to preach" and "to teach" suggest that a major methodology of the church to convey the Good News is to share it by word of mouth.

However, we must go beyond the telling of the gospel. We must demonstrate the teachings and principles of truth given to us in the word of God. "Indeed, the gospel records make it abundantly clear that you cannot separate, in the evangelistic ministry of Jesus, proclamation and demonstration, preaching and acting, saying and doing."[7] The implication for the church is that the "church is called to be an extension of its Lord's incarnation, compassionately responsive to the needs of hurting people."[8] Although we must be careful not to substitute social action for the disciple making imperative of our Lord, compassionate and caring ministry in the name of Jesus is certainly a true expression of the mission of the church.

I would also urge the consideration of the word "represent" as necessary to a proper understanding of the role of the church as it conveys the gospel to the world. To some degree, the church is to represent the will of God for his world as believers live out the implications of the Good News in society. This is more than a demonstration of the meaning of the gospel; it is an embodiment of the will of God in the life of the church. In a unique way, the church conveys the gospel of Christ as the Holy Spirit acts within the body of believers empowering them and setting them free "to serve the living God, to form a new community, to create a new way of life and to proclaim a new message."[9] It is the creating of the new humanity, the new community, the people of God, that is itself shaped and formed by God to represent what God wills to do in all persons and in all of human society. The church is to represent the transforming power of the gospel in its very life.

Thus the church conveys the "good news" of the saving and redeeming activity of God as it declares the truth of God. A centripetal force calls persons to participate in the body of believers as learners. A centrifugal force also sends out the believers to proclaim and demonstrate the truth to the world.[10]

Some distinction needs to be made between the church and the concept of the kingdom of God. While the church is certainly the instrument of God for fulfilling the will of God in our world, the kingdom of God is a larger, more inclusive, thought. In the New Testament, the kingdom of God is present whenever and wherever the rule of God is manifest. "The kingdom of God is the spiritually qualitative existence in which God's rule is acknowledged, loved, and obeyed by rational creatures and His presence is supreme and worshiped."[11]

3. The Church Must Seek God's Vision for Its Mission and Then Adjust Its Life and Ministry to Fit That Vision.

If the church rightly understands the saving activity of God in Christ and acknowledges that God has made the church central to the divine plan for communicating the Good News, then the local body of believers must be willing to shape its life according to God's plan for them. The instruction of Jesus was to "seek first his kingdom and his righteousness and all these things will be given to you as well" (Matthew 6:33). The concerns of the kingdom should take priority over all other temporal concerns. In fact, "the Kingdom makes an absolute demand: we either seek it first or not at all. Having accepted the prior claim of the Kingdom, we then discover the generosity of God."[12] In order to follow the vision of God for the local congregation, "the church must convey to members the deep and sustained conviction that reaching people and making new disciples is supremely important."[13] The mission of the church becomes the source and motivating factor for every aspect of the congregation's life. Certainly, the local church can undertake a multitude of worthy activities and ministries which will contribute to the well being of the congregation and community. The first order of business must be to gauge the value of each activity on the basis of its ability to assist the congregation in accomplishing the mission task. A well balanced approach to nurture and fellowship within the body of believers should compliment the mission endeavor. It should not, however, become a first priority to the exclusion of evangelism and outreach. One of the marks of the true church is that mission is characteristic of its life.[14]

A danger that threatens the effective mission of the local congregation is the slippery slide into the maintenance mode of life. Simply maintaining the existence of a fellowship of believers is not worthy of the calling of our Lord to the church. The real challenge is for the church to increase in strength and vitality while looking outward to its mission. Keeping the mission task of the church central to its life with a deep sense of urgency to fulfill the vision of God should be the aim of the congregation. There is the possibility that like ancient Israel we may miss the real purpose of our calling as the people of God.

Israel's consciousness of her election led to an exclusiveness which blinded her to her spiritual responsibilities to the nations. In place of a concern for mission we find the constant drive for preservation and prosperity. Here are warning notes for the church to heed today.[15]

Shaping the life of the church to be on mission for God may mean some organizational matters that are not necessary to achieving the mission may need to be terminated. In addition, we are reminded that some churches

have complete sets of concrete, cultural practices which they regard as almost synonymous with the gospel. Their witness to Christ is frozen into cultural forms which are irrelevant or unintelligible to most people. They become museum churches with period lifestyles, music, dress and vocabulary. Evangelism for these believers carries all this cultural baggage.[16]

Being on mission for God will include a continual reformation of congregational life and ministry so that the church can be a clear channel of communication for the gospel.

4. The Church on Mission May Justifiably Expect That God Will Provide Kingdom Growth.

When the congregation has sincerely sought to live out God's vision for the church, it can expect the blessing of God as he provides kingdom growth. While all church growth may not be authentic kingdom growth, the church which seeks first the kingdom of God may experience the generosity of God even as it gives itself away in mission and ministry. Indeed, the parables of Jesus regarding the kingdom are replete with the theme of growth. The kingdom news may appear to be insignificant, but it will become great and pervasive in due time. Growth of the kingdom is a strong theme in the gospels.[17]

Increase was undeniably the experience of the early church as it proclaimed the story of God's saving love in Christ. "And the Lord added to their number daily those who were being saved" (Acts 2:47). It is apparent even in a casual reading of the book of Acts that the spread of the Good News is the journal of the expansion of the kingdom.

If there was one unvarying characteristic of apostolic preaching, it was that a verdict was expected. The apostles were forthright in their conviction that God commanded men to repent (Acts 17:30). And they looked for results.[18]

A study of the New Testament images of the church also yields an understanding of the church as an organism that is growing, building, and expanding.[19] However, it is important to state clearly that growth and increase are not the result of human endeavor but are the gift of God. The Apostle Paul called this to the attention of the Corinthian church which was in a leadership conflict. The Corinthian church needed proper instruction about the place of human endeavor. Speaking of this dynamic relationship, Paul wrote, "I planted the seed, Apollos watered it, but God made it grow. So neither he who plants nor he who waters is anything, but only God, who makes things grow" (1 Corinthians 3:6,7).

The essential concept in a proper understanding of God's intention for the church is that the ultimate purpose of all endeavor is to glorify God. The aim of our mission must be to bring glory to the Father.[20] Without question, it should be the intense yearning of the church to glorify God and convey the gospel in the power of the Holy Spirit so that men and women will come to faith in Christ.[21] This is a characteristic of the church on mission.

5. The Church on Mission Seeks to Remove the Impediments so That God May Bring Growth to His Church and Kingdom.

The indispensable task of the church is to cooperate with the design of God for man's salvation. When we acknowledge that it is the will of God for all persons to come into a personal saving relationship with Christ, and that it is God who gives growth to his kingdom through the church, then it becomes necessary for us to remove the impediments and hindrances that we as people may erect to the working of God in our world. If growth is the work of God, then it becomes our task to eliminate any barriers to the working of God through the church. While this may be a rather negative and sometimes puzzling concept, the fact remains that our human characteristics and tendencies often become impediments to the growth of the kingdom. Our task is often to remove the impediments that are so characteristic of human social organization (which includes the assembly of the people of God) to allow the Holy Spirit to work freely among those who are confronted with the gospel.

While we ascribe all ultimate causes of growth to the Holy Spirit, church growth takes place in history and within human society. On the human level, therefore, it develops according to principles, procedures, patterns and methods that conform to human cultural and societal movements.[22]

This will involve dedicated men and women in an ongoing study of the implications of human behavior and groups for the propagation of the gospel. To base our mission and ministry on the insights of sociology and anthropology would be a miscarriage of God's intention. These studies, though valuable, cannot be the basis for the church's outreach. The insights from these areas of study can, however, inform our theology and ministry to provide an understanding which would help us to avoid behaviors which hinder the work of God through the church. This, then, requires us to remove as many hindrances as humanly possible by the practical application of study and experience so that God may work among people unencumbered by our idiosyncracies, tendencies and preferences.

> *Since most of Christianity's objectives for people are achieved in regard to personalities who live in societies, such comfortable isolation from behavioral and social sciences is a luxury that the Christian mission can no longer afford.*[23]

It will be increasingly important for the church which earnestly desires to serve God to the maximum to learn from the study of human behavior how to best facilitate the sharing of the gospel of the kingdom. Ordering church life and the mission endeavor by applying this knowledge to its plans and strategies will have the effect of removing human barriers to the working of the Holy Spirit.

6. *The Empowering of the Holy Spirit is Essential for the Church's Mission and Ministry.*

The instruction of our Lord to those early disciples was a command that is appropriate for the church today.

> *Do not leave Jerusalem, but wait for the gift my Father promised....in a few days you will be baptized with the Holy Spirit. But you will receive power when the Holy Spirit comes on you; and you will be my witnesses in Jerusalem, and in all Judea and Samaria, and to the ends of the earth* (Acts 1:4,5,8).

The empowering of the church by the Holy Spirit is a prerequisite to any authentic endeavor by individuals or the corporate body of believers to fulfill the great commission and be effective in kingdom growth. This empowerment moves the well-intentioned action of men and women beyond mere human activity into the sphere of genuine kingdom mission and ministry. When the Holy Spirit empowers and guides the efforts of the church, then the methods that are used fade into insignificance. Although concerned persons must give attention to the matters that may impede the working of God among people, the fundamental con-

cept is that God gives kingdom growth and the church is but an instrument through which God has chosen to work.
The Holy Spirit is the divine agent to initiate, supervise, energize, and accomplish the purpose of God in the church-building program. Accordingly the church becomes the primary agent of the Paraclete to execute and accomplish the purpose of God.[24]

It is quite important for us to acknowledge this truth because it is a human tendency to begin to trust the skills and methods that are employed in the mission task of the church rather than the Holy Spirit. A proper doctrine of the church will lead us to the conclusion that the church is not just a human institution or organization. Rather it is an organism ordained and empowered by God at Pentecost. As such, the kingdom endeavor is not accomplished by the superior skills, techniques or methods that we might employ.[25]

It is the design of God that individuals and the church be empowered by the Holy Spirit to do the work of God. "This is the great purpose of God's gift to us: to make us more effective in our witness and evangelism."[26] Every aspect of the church's life and ministry must have its source in the dynamic of the Spirit. The Spirit of God imparts spiritual life to the church's life and fellowship, witnessing and preaching. Without the power of God energizing the community of believers individually and corporately, the church will not be effective in sharing the Good News of the kingdom so that men and women are brought to new life in Christ.[27]

One of the major benefits of the Spirit to the church is the gifting of persons for the work of the church.
There are different kinds of gifts, but the same Spirit. There are different kinds of service but the same Lord. There are different kinds of working, but the same God works all of them in all men. Now to each one the manifestation of the Spirit is given for the common good (1 Corinthians 12:4-7).

The understanding that the Holy Spirit equips persons for the church's mission and ministry is a concept that is growing in acceptance in the church at large. It has many implications for the mobilizing of the church to accomplish its mission and ministry.

7. *The Local Church Must Be United in a Primary Mission Objective to Be the Instrument of God in Fulfilling the Great Commission.*

Although one of the previous foundational concepts highlighted the design of God for the church as the conveyor of the gospel, it is vital that the local church be united in its self-understanding regarding its mission and ministry. To have agreement that the church has a primary responsibility to be an agent of salvation and reconciliation on the basis of the biblical mandate is an essential concept that cannot be assumed. The Great Commission of our Lord to "go make disciples" (Matthew 28:19) must have a focus and a priority that overshadows every other motivation for congregational life. The concern for church growth, kingdom increase and reconciliation ministry must be the thread that brings people together and unites them in God's vision for mission and ministry. As one person expressed this motivation, "The unifying strand is a conviction that lost people must be found, that there are hurting, lonely, dying people around us and that Jesus Christ is the answer."[28]

Since the term "church growth" is often misunderstood or misused to imply only a concern for the addition of more names to the membership list, it is crucial that the definition be stated in broader, more inclusive terms. Even though more extensive implications exist — as we shall see in the next foundational concept — a place to begin our understanding is with this definition. The term "church growth" "means all that is involved in bringing men and women who do not have a personal relationship with Jesus Christ into fellowship with him and into responsible life in the church."[29]

The motivating presence of the Holy Spirit in the life of the local congregation impels believers to complete the mission of our Lord Jesus Christ who came to "seek and to save the lost" (Luke 19:10). The congregation that is united in this view of its purpose and is faithful to carry it out may expect the blessing of God in fruitfulness and growth. "The Church which is true to its mandate is one which grows numerically."[30]

8. *Discipleship Does Require Submission to the Lordship of Christ and Obedience to the Demands of the Gospel.*

Whether we address the call to discipleship from the standpoint of the individual or the local congregation, it is imperative that we understand discipleship as more than receiving the benefits of redemption. To accept the redeeming love of Christ must of necessity lead to the demands of the Lordship of Christ. Incorporation into the body of Christ brings a person into a community which looks to the risen Lord as the head of the church. He sets the agenda for the people of God. This does mean that kingdom priorities and the ministry of reconciliation may take the church in unanticipated paths as it follows the instruction to "continue to work out your salvation with fear and trembling" (Philippians 2:12). When we proclaim Jesus as Lord and accept him as "our" Lord, we will find the church moving out in ever-widening circles of mission and ministry. To accept the Lordship of Jesus is to accept the mission of our Lord.[31]

The church that yields its life to the headship of Christ will find a unique role in the plan of God. It will find

> *that its task is to point beyond itself and not to indulge in self-glorification; that to be truly the church it must submit to the Lordship of Christ and live its daily life in dependance on the presence and resources of the Holy Spirit; and that it must be incarnated in the world Christ came to redeem, in which he is already present, and for which he has prepared a transformed future.*[32]

The mission and ministry of the congregation will be shaped by its submission to the whole plan of God for bringing reconciliation and new life to the world. Instead of being molded by the concern for organizational structure and authority, the church under the Lordship of Christ will be shaped by a passion for ministry to persons. It will give energy and resources to the compassionate outreach ministries which honor and complete the ministry of Jesus.

> God is concerned, not only with personal salvation and the training of individual disciples, but also with the establishing of his Kingdom on earth. He wants us to become a new society, a living community that will demonstrate, by its new life-style, new values and new relationships, what his purpose is for the world.[33]

Another implication for the local congregation as it seeks the Lordship of Christ is the quality of life that it develops as a community of believers.

> Probably the most important factor in the witness of a local church is the quality of its corporate life in Christ. Unless a church can proclaim the living Christ, as seen in the united and loving relationships between its members, it has nothing to say apart from empty words and barren theology.[34]

The quality of love within the body of believers is an authentication of the message of reconciliation which we proclaim (John 17:23).

9. *The Church Is Responsible to Mobilize for Mission and Ministry.*

One final foundational concept is necessary for an understanding of God's vision of a people on mission through ministry. An intentional mobilization of the church to conform its life to the divine plan is essential. It would seem that the power of the gospel and the presence of the Holy Spirit in the life of the community of believers would be all that is needed to pursue aggressively the vision that God has for his people. However, the experience of the church has been that seldom has the vitality of mission and ministry been sustained over a long period of time. In every age

God has raised up fresh, dedicated leadership of men and women who have caught God's vision and understood his plan. Then they have given themselves to mobilizing the church to accomplish the mission.

The church is, in reality, people. All too often sinful human nature, the tendency to drift away from the spiritual battle or rely on our own human resources, has nullified the effectiveness of the church on mission. Although the promise of Jesus was that the church would prevail against the powers of evil, it is my conviction that God provides the church with leaders who are gifted by the Holy Spirit to mobilize the whole church for the spiritual warfare. It is then the responsibility of leaders and the entire church intentionally to prepare for and engage in completing the mission and ministry of Jesus in this world.

The mobilization of the church for mission is the responsibility of the entire body of believers. The biblical understanding of the empowering of persons for mission and ministry by the Holy Spirit is at the root of this confidence. Leaders and followers, all God's people, are to be equipped for ministry by the indwelling Spirit. Each person has his or her contribution to make to the growth and effectiveness of the church (Ephesians 4:11-13, 1 Corinthians 12:1-26).

The mobilization of the church is not contrary to the operation of the Spirit in the life of his people. We would affirm that God is a God of order and that planning is not antithetical to guidance of the Holy Spirit.[35] However, it is imperative that the church not substitute human ingenuity or ecclesiastic engineering for the participation of the Spirit in determining the plans of the congregation and church at large. The local congregation through its leaders must accept accountability to God and the church at large to act responsibly in directing the church in accordance with God's vision for his people.

The task of mission, while depending on the empowering and guidance of the Holy Spirit, also requires human planning. The interventions of God do not set aside the need for careful evaluation. The surprises of God are not intended as a substitute for strategy. Responsible decision-making requires well-researched data.[36]

A statement of Kenneth Strachan ought to cause us to think very carefully about the mobilization of the church for mission. "The expansion of any movement is in direct proportion to its success in mobilizing its total membership in continuous propagation of its beliefs. This alone is the key."[37] While this view of the success of movements should not be our only motivation, it should cause the church to be aware that the task cannot be left to a minority of believers or a professional clergy. Indeed, the whole church, every believer, is called to be in the service of the Master and use the gifts of the Spirit to enhance the mission and ministry of the church.[38] The letter of Paul to the Ephesians affirms that when the whole body is working properly it "grows and builds itself up in love, as each part does its work" (Ephesians 4:16).

We are told that the Chinese symbol for the word "crisis" is the combination of the symbols for "danger" and "opportunity." While I would not want to be among the prophets of doom crying out that the church is so ineffective in its mission and ministry that it must be abandoned, I do believe that we are in a crisis situation. The local church is in danger of being consumed by it own internal maintenance concerns. The church out of touch with our culture will be unable to speak or live out the Good News of salvation. It is possible for the local congregation and the church at large to be an enclave of persons only interested in their own welfare and well-being.

The church today has an unparalleled opportunity to be God's people on mission through ministry to this generation. We need a solid theological base and a determination to follow the directives of scripture to obey the call of God. Our task is not to develop our own vision of what should be done, but once again take hold of God's vision for his people. When we have made his vision and will our vision for mission and ministry, a reliance on this theological foundation and the present empowering of the Holy Spirit will propel the church into the next century with purpose and resolution.

ENDNOTES

[2] G. Ernest Wright, GOD WHO ACTS (London: S C M Press, 1952), 44, 55, 66.

[3] Ibid., 57.

[4] Charles Van Engen, THE GROWTH OF THE TRUE CHURCH (Amsterdam: Rodopi, 1981), 117.

[5] Eddie Gibbs, I BELIEVE IN CHURCH GROWTH (Grand Rapids, Michigan: William B. Eerdmans Publishing Company), 26.

[6] Ibid., 34.

[7] David Watson, I BELIEVE IN EVANGELISM (Grand Rapids, Michigan: William B. Eerdmans Publishing Company, 1976), 28.

[8] George G. Hunter III, TO SPREAD THE POWER (Nashville: Abingdon Press, 1987), 137.

[9] George W. Peters, A THEOLOGY OF CHURCH GROWTH (Grand Rapids, Michigan: Zondervan Publishing House, 1981), 140.

[10] Van Engen, 157.

[11] Peters, 40.

[12] Gibbs, 71.

[13] Donald McGavran and George G. Hunter III, CHURCH GROWTH: STRATEGIES THAT WORK (Nashville: Abingdon, 1980), 57.

[14] Van Engen, 106.

[15] Gibbs, 9.

[16] Ray Bakke, THE URBAN CHRISTIAN (Downers Grove, Illinois: InterVarsity Press, 1987), 57.

[17] Van Engen, 425.

[18] Arthur F. Glasser, "An Introduction to the Church Growth Perspectives of Donald Anderson McGavran," ed. Harvey Conn, THEOLOGICAL PERSPECTIVES ON CHURCH GROWTH (Phillipsburg, New Jersey: Presbyterian and Reformed Publishing Co., 1976), 33.

[19] Van Engen, 426.

[20] John M. L. Young, "The Place and Importance of Numerical Church Growth," ed. Harvie Conn, THEOLOGICAL PERSPECTIVES ON CHURCH GROWTH (Phillipsburg, New Jersey: Presbyterian and Reformed Publishing Co., 1976), 62.

[21] Van Engen, 451.

[22] Peters, 20.

[23] Hunter, 15.

[24] Peters, 17.
[25] Ibid., 52.
[26] Watson, 169.
[27] Ibid., 170.
[28] Charles Arn, quoted in C. Wayne Zunkel, CHURCH GROWTH UNDER FIRE (Scottdale, Pennsylvania: Herald Press, 1987), 65.
[29] C. Peter Wagner, YOUR CHURCH CAN BE HEALTHY (Nashville: Abingdon Press, 1979), 14.
[30] Van Engen, 379.
[31] Ibid., 175.
[32] Gibbs, 83.
[33] Watson, 135.
[34] Ibid., 137.
[35] Gibbs, 392.
[36] Ibid., 135.
[37] McGavran and Hunter, 62.
[38] Glasser, 27.

CHAPTER THREE
THE VISION THEME: GOD'S PEOPLE ON MISSION THROUGH MINISTRY

TO BE GOD'S PEOPLE!

A new vision of what the church is to be and do in our world must begin with an understanding of who we are. While that self-understanding may not be shared by everyone who is acquainted with the local congregation, it is critically important that each church have a firm conviction regarding its identity. If church leaders are unsure and timid about "who we are," certainly "what we do" will be of little consequence.

It is impossible to read the pages of the biblical record without stumbling across the profound idea that God is in the business of shaping a people of his own. From the earliest promises given to the patriarchs, God pledged a special relationship with the people he had chosen. They were to be a people set apart as God's own.

For you are a people holy to the Lord your God. The Lord your God has chosen you out of all the peoples on the face of the earth to be his people, his treasured possession (Deuteronomy 7:6).

The Lord will establish you as his holy people, as he promised you on oath, if you keep the commands of the Lord your God and walk in his ways (Deuteronomy 28:9).

The New Testament writers picked up this theme as the expression of the new relationship between the followers of Jesus and God. It was celebrated as a unique and special action of God in his continuing redemptive activity in the world. "But you are a chosen people, a royal priesthood, a holy nation, a people belonging to God, that you may declare the praises of him who called you out of darkness into his wonderful light," (1 Peter 2:9).

At the very heart of our vision for the church ought to be the abiding commitment and confidence that we are God's people, a people belonging to God. This "who we are" statement becomes the foundation of what we are to "be" and "do."

Lest we become puffed up about our name or get drawn into a spiritual snobbishness, we would be well advised to think carefully about the tremendous responsibility attached to the identification as "God's people." Consider implications that have an impact life together in the local church.

The "people" indicates the artificial divisions that we sometimes construct are not what God has in mind for us. The biblical word "laos" which we translate as "people" is inclusive. No separation exists between pastor and people. All are ministers. All have a calling of God. All Christians are to be saints. All are to be priests or "bridge builders" to God. Yes, there are different gifts furnished by the Holy Spirit. Yes, there are different functions and responsibilities, but every believer has a place in the "people of God."

The origin of God's people is very clear. God's people are those persons whom God has "chosen" and "called...out of darkness." God has formed this band of committed believers into a "people" because they have responded to the call of God.

Ownership is unquestioned. The church is a "people belonging to God." We are a servant people who are to do the bidding of our Lord. The final authority for our life and activity is the word of God. We are a community which conforms to the direction and mandates of the Master.

The character of the "people" is unique. We are to be a "holy nation" and "royal priesthood." This is no ordinary group of citizens. We are to stand apart from the customary in our relationship to God and the world.

The purpose for this "people" is very focused. We are to "declare the praises of him who called you out of darkness into his wonderful light" (1 Peter 2:9). The task of the church is to magnify God and give witness to the transformation that he has given to his "people."

The biblical understanding of the "people of God" may be distorted and abused by those who refuse to live as "worthy of the high calling of God." However, true belief and the genuineness of our relationship with God will be known in the fruitfulness of the church as it fulfills God's intended purpose. God's people are not called to special privilege or advantage. God's people are summoned to extraordinary service and ministry.

A verse of scripture which comes to mind as I think about the church and what it is to "be" and "do." The Apostle Paul describes the ministers of the new covenant with these words.

> But thanks be to God, who always leads us in triumphal procession in Christ and through us spreads everywhere the fragrance of the knowledge of him. For we are to God the aroma of Christ among those who are being saved and those who are perishing. To the one we are the smell of death; to the other, the fragrance of life. And who is equal to such a task? (2 Corinthians 2:14-16).

God has called us to be his people. This is an awesome opportunity and responsibility. That will demands our highest commitment.

TO BE ON MISSION FOR GOD

A renewed vision of God's will for his people compels us to move beyond self-understanding. There is much more to our reason for being than just the quality of our relationship with God. Yes, we are identified with him. We affirm with our whole being that we are to be his people, but we must also do his purpose.

We are a people with a purpose. That purpose is not determined by the latest fad or trend line. It is determined by God's directive revealed to us in his written word, the Bible. Indeed, our purpose as a people of God is the very purpose of Jesus who came "to seek and save the lost," (Luke 19:10). We, too, are charged to complete the redeeming activity of God in our world.

The definition of that charge is bold and demanding. Jesus, himself, gave us the urgency and scope of the commission.

"All authority in heaven and on earth has been given to me. Therefore go and make disciples of all nations, baptizing them ...teaching them to obey everything I have commanded you" (Matthew 28:18-20).

If we take this as being our Great Commission, then we must recognize and accept several important aspects of our charge.

1. The commission is given on the basis of the authority of Jesus. The authority to carry out the will of the Father had been given to Jesus. In this statement he bases his charge to his disciples on that authority. "Therefore go...."
2. This is fundamentally an action statement. We are to "go and make disciples" and this will involve us in baptizing and teaching. "Who we are" is translated into a plan to achieve the objectives.
3. The singular goal of the "going" is to "make disciples." The disciple-making task is at the very heart of the command of Jesus. Other tasks and activities are essential, but the focus is on making disciples.

Our problem is that often we know all too well what is expected of us. Our apathy and lack of passion allow us to settle for what is comfortable and non-threatening. Being "at ease in Zion" is often more important to us than pleasing the one who calls us into his service.

Some writers have referred to the "lukewarmness" of the church toward the mission of God on earth as "Saint John's syndrome." The reference is to the word of God through the Apostle John to the church in Ephesus.

I know your deeds, your hard work and your perseverance. You have persevered and have endured hardships for my name, and have not grown weary. Yet I hold this against you: You have forsaken your first love (Revelation 2:2a,3,4).

Those are hard words. This church had been diligent. It had not been lazy; it had endured hardship and persecution. Yet, as the time passed, devotion to Christ had eroded to become cold and passionless. I suspect that many good deeds and efforts had gotten side-tracked from the main purpose. This church had lost its way in the thick of thin things.

One of the greatest dangers that the church faces today is the loss of essential purpose. We can be so consumed with the doing of many good and beneficial secondary activities that we never get to the central task of the church: "Go ... make disciples...."

If we are to be "God's people on mission," our purpose and priorities will be constantly tested against the mission of Jesus and his commission to us. We will need to ask such questions as: "What is our real purpose for existence?" "What kind of a church does God want us to be?" "What business are we in?" "What are we responsible for accomplishing?" "Who is God expecting us to reach for him?"

When the local congregation begins to grapple seriously with such questions relating to the central task of the church, persons will be forced to go beyond the "what's in it for me" mentality. A strictly fellowship orientation to the life and ministry of the church is not compatible with the commission of Jesus.

The church does not exist for its own comfort. It exists primarily as God's agent to share the message of love and redemption with a lost and wayward people. The church has the responsibility for communicating the hope and light of the "good news" in a despairing and dark world.

The church "on mission" will be forced outside of the safety of the fortress to engage the enemy on his territory. The task will be to carry the arena of action out of the sanctuary to the persons and systems enslaved by the power of evil. With the authority of Jesus and the power of his presence, God's people are sent to "do" the mission task. "As the Father has sent me, I am sending you" (John 20:21).

TO BE SERVING PERSONS WITH THE MINISTRY OF CHRIST

The framework for an authentic vision of what the church is to "be" and "do" must of necessity reflect the person and character of Jesus. The focus for our activity and life together in the body of believers is ministry to persons. In essence, we are to become the living reality of the spirit and ministry of our Lord in the actual day-to-day contact with the people about us.

In short, the church should be the embodiment of Jesus in the world. We should be the symbol of his presence; we should be the tangible evidence of the Good News that he brings to the world.

The task of being the real presence of Jesus in our world is an awesome responsibility. The truth is that no individual can attain that lofty goal. No human effort organized through our collective life could ever measure up to the standard that Jesus gave in his love and caring for people. Therein, however, lies the power of God for his work in the world.

The Apostle Paul saw this clearly when he wrote:
Therefore, since through God's mercy we have this ministry, we do not lose heart. But we have this treasure in jars of clay to show that this all-surpassing power is from God and not from us (2 Corinthians 4:1,7).

The ministry of Jesus, sharing the "good news" of God's grace and hope, is neither an impossible task nor a burden to carry beyond our strength. It is the privilege of being called by God to complete the work of Christ through his power. It is the opportunity to be "plugged in" to the source of supernatural strength which compels us to follow in the "footsteps" of Jesus however imperfect that following may be.

The danger that seems to be always with us as we work out the implications of our discipleship is that we often forget "people." In an attempt to "do" the work of Christ, we sometimes become engrossed with the accomplishment of the task to the point of forgetting that "people" are the real focus of ministry. The hurts and pain of persons whom God loves are the real issues whether those be spiritual, emotional or physical in nature.

The call to renewal in the church, to be God's people on mission, must have as its central motivation the healing and health of people. The focus is rightfully on the human component and not on the institutional or "cause" component. So, no matter how true we are to the "truth" or "showy" in our display of "religiosity," the true measure of our discipleship is ministry to people.

Jesus taught, "I tell you the truth, whatever you did for one of the least of these brothers of mine, you did for me" (Matthew 25:40). The Apostle Paul confessed, "If I speak in the tongues of men and of angels, but have not love, I am only a resounding gong or a clanging cymbal" (1 Corinthians 13:1).

The very fabric of the New Testament is woven together with the concept of ministry. While several words are translated in various forms to express "service" or "ministry," none are more compelling than the word *diakonia*. To serve or to minister in the name of Christ is to have a special identity with the ministry of Jesus.

Jesus is our model and mentor. "...whoever wants to become great among you must be your servant...." "For even the Son of Man did not come to be served, but to serve, and to give his life as a ransom for many" (Mark 10:43,45).

This runs counter to our inclination and to the consumerism of American society. The desire for personal power over people and our surroundings seems to be generic for all of us. Nevertheless, the way of Christ to power is the way of the servant.

We are commissioned to a ministry to people in the world.

All this is from God, who reconciled us to himself through Christ and gave us the ministry of reconciliation: that God was reconciling the world to himself in Christ, not counting men's sins against them. And he has committed to us the message of reconciliation (2 Corinthians 5:19,20).

If we have been reconciled to God, the task of reconciliation falls upon us. We are to carry the message and do the service of reconciliation in our world. God is making his appeal through us (2 Corinthians 5:20).

It is God's plan to equip the church for ministry and service through his gifting of leaders.

It was he who gave some to be apostles, some to be prophets, some to be evangelists, and some to be pastors and teachers, to prepare God's people for works of service, so that the body of Christ may be built up until we all reach the unity in the faith and in the knowledge of the Son of God and become mature, attaining the whole measure of the fullness of Christ (Ephesians 4:11-13).

In addition to "doing ministry" in the name of Christ, the primary function of leaders in the church, in this instance pastors and teachers, is to equip God's people for ministry. That is, pastors must give their energies to preparing all disciples for their ministry. This has tremendous implications for our priorities and commitments in the local congregation.

Ministry expresses a commitment to mutual support within the body of believers. "Each one should use whatever gift he has received to serve others, faithfully administering God's grace in its various forms" (1 Peter 4:10).

The building up of the body of Christ for effectiveness is achieved by God through the great variety of gifts and abilities he bestows for the common good (1 Corinthians 12:7). The enablement of the church to do the work of Christ comes through individuals who minister to one another. There are no lone rangers in this kingdom. Personal care giving and support for each other should be the character of this family.

"Ministry" sums up the mission of the church to meet the needs of people, among believers and in society, in the manner of Jesus. We are the bearers of hope to the lost and the least. We are a community of caring people focused outward toward each other.

The vision of the church as GOD'S PEOPLE ON MISSION THROUGH MINISTRY is powerful in its intent and rich in its potential. To wholeheartedly follow this ideal can bring us to the new century with renewed purpose and the blessing of God. It is worthy of our intense energy in this venture of faith.

CHAPTER FOUR
WHAT IS YOUR VISION?

I see a new wind blowing in the church — an awakening across the movement. – Rolland Daniels

If God were here today, I believe he'd be walking the streets of his neighborhood and he'd ask everybody else to do the same. He would probably kick a lot of people out of their structures and "say get out in the streets and do your thing." – Pauline George

We're calling people out today just as we were calling them out a hundred years ago. We're calling them out of sin and calling them into a new life in Jesus Christ. And that's what the Church of God is all about. – Robert Moss

The Lord is interested in giving power and authority and success to wherever his church is located if we follow his direction and do it the way he wants us to. You've got to do God's work God's way. – Jack Eitelbuss

These challenging statements come from pastors and leaders in a video calling the Church of God to a new "Vision 2 Grow." [39] The call to a fresh vision, new understandings of God's will for the church, is at the heart of renewal for the church.

A crucial question for every leader, pastors and lay persons alike, is "What is your vision?" In other words, "What do you perceive to be the calling of God upon the church?" What is God's design for the church? Why do we exist? What is our purpose? What is it that God expects of his people? These are questions to trouble and make us restless with the often comfortable, complacent, business-as-usual state of the church.

Indeed, the inquiry is personal! What is your vision? An individual may retreat from personal responsibility by dumping the probing question upon the church in general or a pastor or other leadership. Comments like, "The church doesn't seem to know where it is heading" may be an attempt to avoid our personal accountability. By complaining that the church doesn't have a clear purpose or direction, we may be indicting ourselves. After all, who is the church? The church is all of God's people who are engaged in fulfilling the call of God. Vision, therefore, is both a personal and corporate responsibility. We are all involved in this venture! In this aspect of the life of the church, we really do need each other.

The concept of "vision" certainly is not new or novel, but it is critical. In both the Old and New Testaments, God speaks to men and women in visions. These were encounters with God or the truth of God. Through special manifestations, God imparted knowledge of circumstances and events. The importance of the vision was that it was a means whereby God imparted an understanding of himself or human situations. Through this special revelation, men and women came to know God and his will for his people.

The events surrounding the call and mission of the Apostle Paul clearly illustrate the place of vision in the biblical literature. On the road to Damascus, Saul, the persecutor of the Lord's disciples, was literally struck down by the blazing light from heaven. The instructions from the risen Lord left him confused, and in his blinded condition he could reach the city only with the assistance of fellow travelers.

However, God communicated his plan by a vision through Ananias.

In Damascus there was a disciple named Ananias. The Lord called to him in a vision, "Ananias!" "Yes, Lord," he answered. The Lord told him, "Go to the house of Judas on Straight Street and ask for a man from Tarsus named Saul, for he is praying. In a vision he has seen a man named Ananias come and place his hands on him to restore his sight" (Acts 9:10 - 12).

Not only did the Apostle change his direction of life as a result of this encounter with God and the ministry of Ananias, but this experience became the driving force which motivated him to fulfill his calling. In his defense before Agrippa, Paul's testimony was strong. "So then, King Agrippa, I was not disobedient to the vision from heaven" (Acts 26:19).

When we engage in a discussion of vision in biblical literature, we usually become engrossed in the "means" of the vision — how it occurred and the situation that it explained. However, God's intent in giving the vision was to disclose his divine will.

That is the true function of vision for the church today. To be effective as "God's people on mission through ministry," we must discern what his will is for us as a people and what he desires us to do for him. That is the essence of vision.

A dictionary definition of vision is also instructive when we think about vision as a concept for the church. The American College Dictionary describes one aspect of vision as "the act or power of perceiving what is not actually present to the eye, whether by some supernatural endowment or by natural intellectual acuteness."[40] Translated into kingdom terms: Our vision of the church's ministry is the ability to perceive what God wants done in and through the church as we think through the implications of the Great Commission and seek his guidance in the tasks to fulfill his will.

I embrace a more personal definition of vision. Vision, for me, is a mental/spiritual image of a preferable future rooted in the person and plan of God, and in understanding our finite limitations and capacity.[41] That is, we are able to visualize what God expects to do in us and through us on the basis of our faith in God (his infinite possibility) and our spiritual giftedness (our limited but God-given abilities). Faith in God is the resource for an expanding view of our potential while our limited capacity is the reason for defining our priorities.

A working definition of vision which is precise, inclusive and carefully crafted has become the basis for a new understanding of how God communicates his will and design to his people through his leaders. "Vision for ministry is a clear mental image of a preferable future, imparted by God to his chosen servants, based upon an accurate understanding of God, self, and circumstances."[42]

Canon John Finney, however, has observed that most churches do not shape their ministry by means of a vision of what God is calling them to be and do.[43] Rather, he suggests that many are circular in behavior. That is, their life together is constructed by the circular pattern of the annual program. They often fall into a habit of doing once again what they did the previous year. They may raise the budget or project some expectation of a new development in their ministry. More often than not, however, it is a downward spiral, afflicted with the deadly sameness of the events year after year.

Other congregations are event oriented. Finney refers to these as fire-cracker churches.[44] They are motivated and driven by the high energy occasions which demand the time and involvement of many persons. These are the churches where something is always happening. So the history of the congregation, whether of success or failure, can be charted by the large and small events which remain in the memory of the faithful.

A third possible mode of operation is found among churches influenced by the writings of Peter Drucker to adopt the principles of "management by objectives (MBO)."[45] These are "directional" churches which formulate their ministry on the basis of goals and objectives. While this approach is certainly preferable to the "haphazard" non-direction of many churches, Finney is critical of the rigid MBO doctrine for congregations.[46] It tends to fall short in the actual life of most congregations in that goals set by the minister or a group in the church may not be fully achievable or appropriate for the group with the passing of time.

The will of God, however, captured in the vision imparted by God should be the driving force for the collective ministry of the congregation. Just as with the Hebrew nation, vision is like the cloud by day and the pillar of fire by night for the church. "Without the pillar or cloud, we wander aimlessly in the desert."[47]

In the blockbuster book **WITHOUT A VISION, THE PEOPLE PERISH**, George Barna declares a solid link between the shared vision within the local church and its effectiveness in growth and ministry.

In every one of the growing, healthy churches I have studied, there is a discernible link between the spiritual and numerical growth of those congregations and the existence, articulation, and widespread ownership of God's vision for ministry by the leaders and participants of the church. Conversely, there is invariably a clear absence of vision in those congregations in which there is neither spiritual nor numerical growth taking place. Rarely in my research do I find such overt, black-and-white relationships.[48]

Recent literature confirms the importance of vision for any organization. Those findings are especially crucial for the local congregation. The generating of vision is the "creating of focus" for the life of the group.[49] "Vision animates, inspirits, transforms purpose into action."[50]

In addition to the strong motivation that captures persons, shared vision has the capacity to involve individuals in the enterprise in a way that is fulfilling.

When the organization has a clear sense of its purpose, direction, and desired future state and when this image is widely shared, individuals are able to find their own roles both in the organization and in the larger society of which they are a part. This empowers individuals and confers status upon them because they can see themselves as part of a worthwhile enterprise.[51]

This sense of unity and fulfillment in the achieving of God's design is decisive in the life of the local congregation.

When persons committed to the Lordship of Jesus Christ see clearly the reason and objective for church and are willing to wholeheartedly give themselves to this design, the result is great strength of purpose. The conflicts that are typical of church life are minimized. The sense of accomplishment, aligned with the truth of God's Word, is compelling and ultimately worth the time and energy expended. The church that lives according to its shared vision has the potential of changing the lives of people and the world.

Futurist Joel Barker in the video **THE POWER OF VISION** has correctly ascribed a "positive vision of the future" as the most important factor to those who are powerfully motivated to "make a difference in the world."[52] In answer to the question "What makes up Vision?" Barker lists four qualities:

1. Visions need to be developed by leaders. That is, leaders bring the vision into a coherent focus so the group understands it.
2. Visions of the leaders must be shared and supported. When there is agreement on direction, a "vision community" is created.
3. Vision must be comprehensive and detailed. When it is specific and complete, each person can participate in fulfilling the vision and contribute creativity and ability to the endeavor.
4. Vision must be positive and inspiring.

His conclusion is that once you have your "vision community," you can accomplish what may have seemed impossible. "We gain through the strength of our vision the power to shape the future."[53] "Vision without action is merely a dream. Action without vision just passes the time. Vision with action can change the world."[54]

While it would be possible for us to dismiss these statements as just hype, the truth is that the local congregation ought to have as much reason for optimism for the future as any group of people in the world. Yes, the obstacles are great, but the church is ordained by God and set apart for his purposes. The local church has the capability of being the most visionary entity today because of its divine purpose and mandate. The difficulty may be that the church and its leaders may be living off the spiritual energy of the past. Often, in this depleted state, the power for being God's people on mission through ministry is pitifully weak.

Barna makes a strong and daring statement.

Realize that vision is the starting point for true ministry. For a Christian leader - that is, an individual chosen by God to move His people forward - vision is not to be regarded as an option. It is the insight that instructs the leader and directs his or her paths. If, for whatever reason, you are attempting to lead God's people without God's vision for your ministry, you are simply playing a dangerous game. It is a game that is neither pleasing to God nor satisfying to man.[55]

In my experience, one of the most painful yet motivating questions that has ever been asked of me was, "What is your vision for the church?" The personal quest to find and understand what God's vision is and to make that "my" vision is an ongoing task. It is the essential task for every leader in the local church!

If we are to be effective in fulfilling the call of God in our personal lives and in the ministry of the local congregation, we must ask the question "What is your vision for the church?" Power and strength will come to the local church when leaders frame their answer in harmony with God's vision — the design and plan of God for their congregation. The result will be "God's people on mission through ministry."

ENDNOTES

[39] VISION 2 GROW VIDEO (Anderson, Indiana: Leadership Council of the Church of God, 1992).

[40] Clarence Barnhart, ed., AMERICAN COLLEGE DICTIONARY (New York: Harper and Brothers Publishers, 1953), 1361.
[41] Jim Dethmer, Pastor's Update Monthly Cassette Program (Pasadena, California: Charles E. Fuller Institute of Evangelism and Church Growth, September 1990), audio cassette.
[42] George Barna, WITHOUT A VISION, THE PEOPLE PERISH (Glendale, California: Barna Research Group Limited, 1991), 28.
[43] John Finney, unpublished seminar notes (Pasadena, California: Fuller Theological Seminary, January 1992).
[44] Ibid.
[45] Ibid.
[46] John Finney, UNDERSTANDING LEADERSHIP (London: Daybreak, 1989), 118-121.
[47] Finney, unpublished seminar notes.
[48] Barna, 12.
[49] Warren Bennis and Burt Nanus, LEADERS: THE STRATEGIES FOR TAKING CHARGE (New York: Harper and Row, Publishers, 1985), 28.
[50] Bennis and Nanus, 30.
[51] Bennis and Nanus, 90,91.
[52] Joel Arthur Barker, THE POWER OF VISION (Burnsville, Minnesota: Charthouse Learning Corporation, 1990), videocassette.
[53] Ibid.
[54] Ibid.
[55] Barna, 16.

CHAPTER FIVE
DEVELOPING A MISSION STRATEGY

Rarely will a flash of inspiration result in — eureka — the local congregation capturing God's vision for the church. Deep conviction, born out of a revelation by the Spirit of God, is the character of vision, but the details take shape over time. Pastors and leaders may expect that vision for the local congregation to spring to life because it is desperately needed and earnestly sought; but in reality, this is unusual.

I've watched congregational vision develop over a period of time with many points of inspiration and insight as well as times of uncertainty and indecision. In other words, vision which becomes the motivating force for congregational life may, indeed, come in the brilliant ray of insight. More often, it is the result of a prayerful quest by church leaders to understand the whole will of God for their lives and ministry. The vision may emerge in the search to be authentically God's people on mission through ministry.

The place to begin the pilgrimage is to look once again at the purpose of the church. What is God's intention for the body of believers?

MISSION PURPOSE

The vision for a congregation's life and ministry will flow out of its concept of God's purpose for the church. Purpose, by its very nature, determines the ends for which the church exists. Purpose answers the "why" question! It focuses on the reasons for being. "The effective church is a body of people who have been 'laid hold of' by one mastering, divine purpose. It is captivated by Christ's mission."[56]

The congregation that seeks renewal by the power of God in its life will of necessity seek a renewal of purpose.

To go beyond mere "existence" and the "maintenance mode," the local church will expend time and energy in searching the scripture and in dialogue to reaffirm the purpose of the church.

The source for this exploration is the Bible. Digging out of the Word, especially the New Testament, the divine purpose will provide the basis for a strategy for the life and ministry of God's people.

There are a multitude of possibilities for a systematic approach to determining the biblical foundation for the mission purpose of the congregation. However, Charles Mylander has suggested that the church has been given four mandates which become the purposes that give direction and guidance for the local congregation.[57]

The Great Commandment - Matthew 22:37
The Great Concern - Matthew 22:39
The Great Commission - Matthew 28:18 - 20
The Great Commitment - John 13:34 - 35

The Great Commandment

To "Love the Lord your God with all your heart and with all your soul and with all your mind" (Matthew 22:37), is the first and greatest commandment. Jesus gave every individual follower and the church this mandate, not so much as an obligation, but as the greatest privilege of a mutual love relationship. First in our affection and first in our priorities, we are to love God with every fiber of our being. Not only does the worship of the church find its source in this commandment, but prayer as the means of communication is rooted in this relationship. "Our Father in heaven, hallowed be your name, your kingdom come, your will be done on earth as it is in heaven," (Matthew 6:10,11).

The Great Concern

A second mandate follows closely on the words of the Master. "Love your neighbor as yourself," (Matthew 22:39).

The love which nourishes the vertical relationship with God is to also have expression in the horizontal relationships with neighbors, even enemies (Matthew 5:44). The great concern, then, is that love modeled in the "agape" of God toward us and in our loving response to God finds release in us and in other persons whom God loves. We are to be conduits of love, God's love in us and through us, to people. This great concern becomes the motivation for sharing the good news of salvation in Jesus. This great concern fuels compassionate ministries. This great concern propels us to seek justice for the poor and dispossessed of our society.

The Great Commission

The words of Jesus to the first disciples to "go and make disciples of all nations, baptizing them ... and teaching them to obey" (Matthew 28:19-20) is our mandate as well as theirs. "Make disciples" is the unmistakable imperative of Jesus and becomes central to the mission purpose. The fundamental task of enlisting and developing "more and better" disciples is under the authority of Jesus. "Go" is an active word signifying an aggressive presence in our communities. "Baptizing" urges us to bring these disciples to a new life in Christ and enfold them in the community of believers. "Teaching them to obey" emphasizes the continuing journey to maturity in the "fullness of Christ."

The Great Commitment

Resident in the New Testament is the challenge of a "called out" people who have a special relationship with each other and with God. They are identified as God's people. "But you are a chosen people, a royal priesthood, a holy nation, a people belonging to God, that you may declare the praises of him who called you out of darkness into his wonderful light" (1 Peter 2:9). That new relationship with God not only results in a mission purpose, but it also carries with it the command of a new commitment. "As I have loved you, so you must love one another. All men will know that you are my disciples if you love one another" (John 13:34,35). In other words, the great commitment of love to the believers in the body of Christ authenticates the genuineness of our discipleship.

This is but one of the many possible scriptural foundations on which the local church may build a mission purpose. It is important that the basis for the mission strategy be broad and comprehensive. This, in fact, is one of the differences that distinguishes "vision" from mission purpose. Mission purpose is by its nature broad and philosophic. Vision, however, is specific and detailed and incorporates the goals as well as the ways and means of accomplishing the purpose.

One young pastor, for example, has focused his preaching and teaching on Acts 2:42 - 47 as an approach for building consensus for the mission purpose of a local congregation. He outlined the passage in such a way that it undergirds the present life of the congregation and also paves the way for an expanded mission strategy.[58]

The purpose of the Minges Hills Church of God is to glorify God by being obedient to His Word, the Bible, in and through the four goals of the church, Acts 2:42 - 47:

1. *Provide for Worship of God.*
   Public and corporate, personal and private
   Romans 12:1, John 4:24

2. *Provide for the Spiritual Maturity of Each Individual.*
   Evangelism, discipleship
   Matthew 28:18 - 20, Acts 1:8, 2 Peter 3:9

3. *Provide for Fellowship.*
   Personal support and encouragement by group involvement
   1 John 1:7, Romans 15:5 - 7, Hebrews 10:23 - 25

4. *Provide the Opportunity for Fulfillment in Service*
Education, training, missions, service
Ephesians 4:11 - 13, Galatians 5:13,
Matthew 25:34 - 40, 1 Peter 4:8 - 11

Developing a mission strategy in the local congregation will depend to a large extent on the ability of leaders and workers in the congregation to accept and support a mission purpose. The mission purpose must not only be rationally understood, it must also become the heart and soul of their belief structure and action plans.

Leadership retreats are excellent opportunities for responsible persons to work through their biblical concepts in dialogue with each other. The personal investment of thought, time and relationship building will reap great rewards as the church moves forward with greater understanding and conviction.

MISSION CONTEXT

Also critical to the development of a mission strategy is knowledge of the mission setting. To capture God's vision for the local congregation means that responsible leaders will apply the biblical purpose for the church to the needs of the community. Unfortunately, many congregations have a clear biblical concept of God's purpose for the church but never relate that to the real needs that surround them. They become isolated and ingrown, ineffective in mission and ministry.

There are several excellent tools available for assisting the local congregation in exploring the context for mission and ministry. These are listed in the "Resources for Further Study" at the end of the chapter and are available at nominal cost.

My purpose is to identify several factors with which each local congregation must grapple if it is to have an effective mission strategy. These are not optional considerations. They are central to the development process.

Know Your Community

An abundance of data is available today which will help inform the local congregation as it makes mission and ministry decisions. Demographic information is now readily available and can be interpreted to give the big people picture of the community. The hard data will include a breakdown of such things as age, marital status, income, race and national origin and an array of statistics that describe the community context for the church's ministry. Trends in the population will appear as they are compared with previous census figures and other communities. Correctly interpreted, the demographic data will identify areas of growth or decline that will have impact on the ministry of the congregation. People who are in transition and life-cycle changes are more apt to be open to the Good News of Jesus Christ and more receptive to the ministry of the church. A congregation may meet the life-cycle needs of persons in the community as it becomes aware of the needs that coincide with the resources and stated purpose of the church.

Resources and tools for the examination of community demographics are listed in "Resources for Further Study" at the end of the chapter. The local church will often have at its disposal persons who are already skilled at this type of inquiry. Persons who are in public-school administration or public-service businesses are often well informed and can supply the data that will benefit the mission strategy of the church.

One crucial piece of community information will be the percentage of the unchurched population. While this statistic may be available through published studies of your community or state (Glenmary Institute), it can be estimated by a rather simple procedure. One method is to calculate the total seating capacity of all the churches that serve community residents. Double that capacity number and then divide by the total population of the community to get a rough estimated percentage of the unchurched persons. This method may not be feasible for metropolitan areas, but usually it results in the realization that there are many, many people in our communities who are untouched by any congregation.

There are today church consultants in every area of the nation who are skilled in community analysis and can provide knowledge to enhance the effectiveness of the local congregation. An example of this valuable assistance occurred early in my ministry as the founding pastor of a congregation in Champaign, Illinois. As a new congregation in a unique community, the leaders struggled over the complex decisions that they were facing. We called on Dr. Val Clear, a sociologist and committed Christian professor at Anderson University, to survey our community. His study saved the congregation from making some disastrous decisions that were being urged upon us by well-meaning but misguided persons. Not only was the consultant cost effective, but his report unified the congregation around a course of action which gave us direction and purpose.

Soft data also exist that the congregation needs as it determines its mission strategy. "Soft" data provide information regarding the attitudes present among people in the community. These attitudes may be a part of the culture of the community and may never appear in the statistical analysis. Lingering opinions, decades old, may become barriers to effective ministry. Wise leaders will seek out and be attentive to the attitudes that are often below the surface.

One means of knowing the character and disposition of a community is to spend time talking to community leaders and residents. Personal interviews with community people unattached to any Christian church may yield information which will creatively shape the ministry of a local congregation. Some new church planters have spent hundreds of hours going from door to door with the intent of learning from residents their needs, their hurts, their hopes and dreams. The testimony of these interviewers is that their conception of what the church ought to be and do was radically changed. To develop a mission strategy on the basis of the life needs of the people in a community and the biblical mandates is to make our mission and ministry relevant.

A body of literature that deals with both the "hard" and the "soft" data is now available to every congregation. The information being written about the "baby boomers" or the "baby busters" or the "aging" is not just for demographers or sociologists. Wise leaders will seek to be informed about the characteristics of people in the congregation's mission area and shape mission strategy accordingly.

Congregational History

Essential to understanding the local congregation's present ministry situation is a diagnostic look at the history of the congregation. The details of the birth and growth of the church are often preserved in written documents prepared for anniversaries or significant events in the life of the congregation. While these facts are valuable for long view, the more pertinent data will deal with the statistics of the past ten years. The record of membership or constituency, church school average attendance and morning worship average attendance for the past eleven years can be graphed to give a picture of the trends. The financial records over this period will also provide information regarding priorities of the congregation and its response to corporate obligations.

Once again, tools and guides to accomplish this task are listed in the section "Resources for Further Study" at the end of the chapter. Although many factors will have impact on the congregation's record of growth or decline, a twenty-five percent growth rate over a decade is considered as less than adequate or "poor" growth. A one-hundred percent growth rate has been judged as "good" while two hundred percent is "excellent." Currently, more than eighty-five percent of existing congregations in North America are either plateaued or declining.

Present Ministry and Worker Analysis

One additional factor is necessary to complete our understanding of the local congregation's context for ministry. An accurate listing of all present ministry activities, the persons involved and worker hours required to carry on each ministry is essential information. Tools and workbooks for this task are listed in the section "Resources for Further Study."

The purpose of this information is to help congregational leaders to analyze the nature and extent of the present ministry effort. It will indicate who is being served in the life of the congregation. It may also reveal significant differences from the community profile. Other gaps and deficiencies may become apparent as the congregation looks seriously at developing a mission strategy.

One important statistic relates to the numerical strength of the workers available for the ministry plan. The numbers of workers presently involved in ministry should be compared with the total adult and youth constituency. The ratio of workers to "consumers," those persons toward whom the ministry is directed, is a sometimes revealing statistic. A target that many consultants recommend is one worker for every "consumer." A worker force of fifty percent of the constituency is a healthy balance. A ratio of less than fifty percent usually indicates an active but struggling congregation or passive and dying church.

A further breakdown of the workers into ministries focused internally to the church body and those focused outward toward the community in evangelism or compassionate ministries will astound most congregational leaders. It is not unusual for leaders to assume that much of the congregation's ministry touches people outside the community of faith. However, in most congregations only a small fraction of the effort and money expended in ministry is directed to those outside the fellowship.

In a survey of twenty-one congregations linked together in a training program in Michigan called "Partnership for Growth," we found that on the average less than five percent of the workers focused their time and effort outside the present attenders. I do not find that unusual for the nominal congregation. However, a mission strategy that directs a greater share of the congregational ministry outward toward the community will take a large step in becoming effective in reaching people for Christ.

The target for volunteer workers in the healthy and growing church is eighty percent for internal ministry and twenty percent for external ministry. The congregation that designates one of every ten committed attenders to ministry in the community will thrive and reproduce through conversion growth.

MISSION STATEMENT

Another component in creating vision and cultivating a vision community is the writing of a mission purpose. The mission statement makes the "reason for being" explicit and has the potential of communicating the purpose to all persons in the congregation. The mission statement gives further clarity to the biblical purpose of the church because it defines the response of the congregation to the mission context. Although mission statements by their nature are broad and encompass the total range of the congregation's ministry, they are specific enough to describe how the church will respond to the needs of the community.

The writing of a mission statement is not a solo endeavor. It is an arduous task to be accomplished by a group of people with different concerns and viewpoints concerning the work and purpose of the church. That measure of difficulty becomes a positive and enriching strength for the mission strategy of the church. Leaders are forced to think and talk through their assumptions regarding the church and its mission and come to some form of consensus and agreement.

The leadership retreat setting is most productive for writing a mission statement because persons must remain in dialogue even though highly volatile disagreements may erupt. Indeed, the building of relationships that can occur in this process is as important as the end product. In my experience, the writing of a mission statement may not be accomplished at one event. It may take additional time for reflection and further study to come to an agreed upon and mutually supported mission statement. In fact, if a congregation has not had in place a productive ongoing planning process or are not comfortable with the "paper and pencil" mode, then wise leaders may need to develop the mission statement over a period of time in smaller incremental steps.

It often aids the active and highly participative congregation to have the pastor or other leader write a proposed mission statement based on the preaching and teaching that has occurred regarding the purpose of the church. Leaders then have a starting point and can suggest additions and objections. In any case, through the developmental stage, all of the ideas and contributions should be weighed and given consideration. Eventually the mission statement should be condensed to not more than three sentences. Two is better. Someone has indicated that mission statements have value in an inverse proportion to their length. In other words, the shorter the better if it is to be remembered and used in the mission strategy planning.

The value of the mission statement will become more apparent over time as it is utilized in the planning process. Often it will assist the congregation by limiting the expansion of ministry into areas which may be outside its purpose. The boundaries that mission statements provide can keep the church from activities and programs that will drain energy and revenue away from the central purpose. Most importantly, the mission statement can become a "hook" on which the local congregation can hang the mission goals in the development of the mission strategy.

MISSION PLANNING

Another major factor in developing a mission strategy for the local congregation is the creation of a continuing circular planning process. A biblical mission purpose and an understanding of the mission setting must be fleshed out in a process that has the potential of bringing renewal to congregational life year after year. When leaders come to endorse a mission purpose for the local congregation and they comprehend how the context for ministry has impact on that mission, then a planning system must be devised to move forward to accomplish the task. The result should be a plan to fulfill the mission purpose.

It should be apparent that to be without a plan is to invite ineffectiveness and disaster. Not to plan is itself a plan. It is a plan to fail to accomplish the mission purpose and God's vision for the congregation. Moreover, to attempt to keep things as they are will inevitably lead to being out of touch with a rapidly changing society. Ineffectiveness in reaching people in need and the decline of a congregation's ministry will be the result. Soon the morale of the church and hope for the future is destroyed. As someone aptly observed, "The 'status quo' is Latin for the 'mess we're in.'"

It is crucial for the congregation which wants to create and maintain mission strategy that the planning process be "circular." That simply means that the process should be designed so that leaders are obligated to revisit the process annually to update their progress. Dayton and Engstrom suggest that the following elements should be incorporated into the annual cycle.[59]

    a. Purpose establishment
    b. Goal setting
    c. Planning
    d. Action

e. Correction
f. Evaluation
g. Renewal of purpose, etc.

Mission Strategy Cycle

Purpose Establishment → Goal Setting → Planning → Action → Correction → Evaluation → (Purpose Establishment)

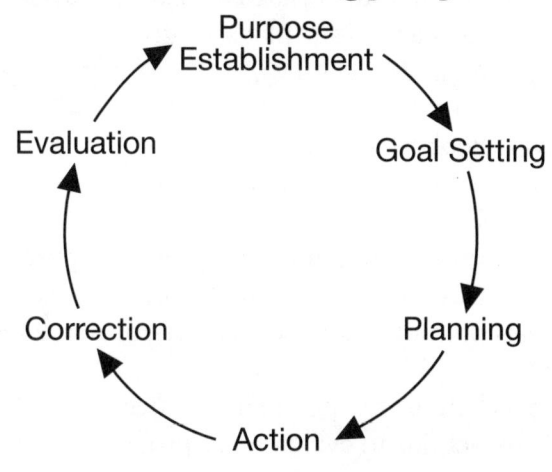

Figure 1. Mission Strategy Cycle.

Planning is the process of getting from where the church is now to where it wants to be. The "vision" of where the church should be comes through leaders able to capture God's vision and purpose for the congregation. They create a "vision community" in the congregation and continually communicate the vision to the larger group. On the basis of the mission purpose and the mission context, the "vision" takes shape as it is lived out in the life of the church. The mission strategy develops out of three elements which move the congregation to accomplish the "vision."

Mission Goal Setting

Goal setting to accomplish the mission of the congregation is a powerful tool in developing a mission strategy. Goals, by their very nature, are statements of faith regarding the future.[60] To project what the congregation will attempt to do in the next three to five years and beyond is to have faith that God is leading the congregation into a significant and productive future. It is to "dream" about the possibilities and believe that God is leading the congregation to a better day for its mission and ministry. "For I know the plans I have for you, declares the Lord, plans to prosper you and not to harm you, plans to give you hope and a future" (Jeremiah 29:11, NIV).

In STRATEGY FOR LEADERSHIP, a book which has become a workbook for many, Dayton and Engstrom list ten reasons for the powerful effect that goal setting has in congregational planning.[61]

1. Goals give a sense of direction and purpose.
2. Goals give us the power to live in the present.
3. Goals promote enthusiasm and strong organizational life.
4. Goals help us to operate more effectively.
5. Goals help us to evaluate our progress.
6. Goals force us to plan ahead.
7. Goals help us to communicate within the organization.
8. Goals give people a clear understanding of what is expected.
9. Goals help us to reduce needless conflict and duplication of effort.
10. Goals take the emphasis off activity and place it on output.

There are, of course, different types of goals. Often categories like long range and short term are used to designate the type of goal. However, of great importance to developing mission strategy is the "strategic" goal. This refers to goals that guide the direction of the mission. They, too, must be specific, measurable and accomplishable within a designated time frame. They are to be distinguished from "tactical" goals which are usually short term and represent interim steps toward the "strategic" goal.

Dayton and Engstrom suggest several characteristics of what they call "operational" goals.[62]
1. A goal should be related in some way to the organization's purposes.
2. We must believe we can do it.
3. A goal should have a date when it will be accomplished.
4. A goal must be measurable.
5. A goal needs to be supported by a plan.
6. A goal needs to be claimed by someone.
7. A goal must be supported by the necessary resources.

In recent years a number of books have been written to guide congregations in understanding and adopting an organizational style in which goal setting becomes a driving force to accomplish the purpose of the congregation. The congregation which is serious about developing a strategy for reaching its vision will take advantage of the resources and incorporate goal setting into its planning process.

Implementation

Once strategic goals have been established, the mission-planning phase moves toward implementation. Initiating action to move toward the goal is crucial. There is nothing magic or automatic about setting goals. They must be implemented with strength if the congregation is to develop the mission strategy.

An action plan becomes necessary for the implementation of goals. Once again, the plan must be written with enough detail and structure to act as a guide in the mission strategy.

A good implementation plan will give information regarding the following:

Strategizing: What activities will we do to reach our goal?
Scheduling: When will each activity take place?

Recruiting and Assigning:	Who is responsible to see that it happens?
Resourcing:	What are the equipment, space, money, and worker needs to carry out the activity?
Monitoring:	How will we check up to be sure the plan is functioning properly and on time?[63]

This phase includes the planning, action and correction portion of the circular process recommended by Dayton and Engstrom. In this part of the process, the goal is assigned to an individual or group responsible to develop action steps, assess what resources are needed, and enlist the people to carry out the goal. While the goal may not originate with those acting upon it, there should be sufficient "ownership" by the implementing person or group to ensure follow through. Accountability for the goal is necessary. However, there is need for freedom and the authority to make mid-course corrections if necessary. Problems do occur in achieving goals and there must be the autonomy and initiative to solve them.

Evaluation

Evaluation must be included in the process of developing a mission strategy. Because we are human and prone to failure and mistakes, there will never be a "perfect" goal or plan which cannot be improved. We can learn from experience and we accept success and failure with equal grace when we are seeking God's will for the congregation.

Unfortunately, many programs begun with high hopes and expectations outlive their effectiveness. The congregation continues to maintain these out of a sense of obligation to the goals of a former day or persons who may have passed off the scene of action. Evaluation of all aspects of congregational life should be made with mission purpose, mission context and mission goals positively and explicitly presented.

Effective congregations are tough-minded in evaluating their efforts and clear-eyed in deciding what to do. They are more concerned with what is effective than what they as individuals may prefer. They are marked by a willingness to do whatever is necessary at whatever the cost.[64]

Developing a strategy for mission in the local congregation is a complex and demanding task. For reasons that we will explore in the next chapter, a mission orientation is not easy for a congregation to achieve. However, if the leaders capture God's vision for the local church and guide the congregation to embrace a biblical purpose, examine their ministry context, write a mission statement and institute a mission planning process, God's plan can be realized. It is possible for every congregation to be God's people on mission through ministry.

RESOURCES FOR FURTHER STUDY AND ACTION

Anderson, Leith. DYING FOR CHANGE. Minneapolis, Minnesota: Bethany House Publishers, 1990.

Dayton, Edward R. and Ted W. Engstrom. STRATEGY FOR LEADERSHIP. Old Tappan, New Jersey: Fleming H. Revell Company, 1979.

Lindgren, Alvin J. and Norman Shawchuck. LET MY PEOPLE GO. Nashville: Abingdon Press, 1980.

Workbooks

COMMUNITY ANALYSIS. Charles E. Fuller Institute of Evangelism and Church Growth, 1981.

GROWTH HISTORY. Charles E. Fuller Institute of Evangelism and Church Growth, 1982.

PASTOR'S PLANNING WORKBOOK. (Part One, Part Two, Part Three, Part Four). Charles E. Fuller Institute of Evangelism and Church Growth, 1981, 1982.

WORKER ANALYSIS. Charles E. Fuller Institute of Evangelism and Church Growth, 1981.

ENDNOTES

[56] Joe S. Ellis, THE CHURCH ON PURPOSE (Cincinnati, Ohio: Standard Publishing, 1982), 20.

[57] Charles Mylander, SECRETS FOR GROWING CHURCHES (San Francisco: Harper and Row, Publishers, 1979), 27-40.

[58] This mission purpose was developed by Reverend Timothy Kumfer, pastor of the Minges Hills Church of God, Battle Creek, Michigan in 1992.

[59] Edward R. Dayton and Ted W. Engstrom, STRATEGY FOR LEADERSHIP (Old Tappan, New Jersey: Fleming H. Revell Company, 1979), 112.

[60] Ibid., 53.

[61] Ibid., 56-58.

[62] Ibid., 63-64.

[63] Alvin J. Lindgren and Norman Shawchuck, LET MY PEOPLE GO (Nashville: Abingdon Press, 1980), 84,85.

[64] Ellis, 22.

CHAPTER SIX
WHEN FELLOWSHIP AND MISSION COLLIDE

The call came early on Monday morning. That was not unusual and the topic of conversation was not surprising. A young pastor was deeply disappointed. He was frustrated and talked of circulating his resume to other congregations that would be more receptive to his style of leadership and his vision for the mission and ministry of the local congregation.

Just two weeks earlier this same young man had described to me in glowing terms the dreams he had shared with the church. The congregation had grown significantly since the arrival of his family and now, after a year of attracting other young families, its facilities were being strained to the limit. In fact, the church had started a new Sunday School class for young marrieds in the parsonage just across the very small parking lot. The class had now surpassed the older adult class in attendance. Not only had the Board of Trustees investigated the possibility of expanding the sanctuary for added worship space, but the basement of the church building was now being remodeled to accommodate larger children's classes. There was even some talk of creating space in the remodeling project for fellowship dinners and social events. However, some persons opposed having "parties" in the church building, but the pastor was confident that when everyone understood the purpose for the social hall it would be approved.

Other plans were projected for ministry in the community, but these were all on hold. In the church's annual meeting several persons had stood to speak in opposition to all of the new procedures and changes that the congregation had experienced in the past year. It was pointed out that the current financial difficulties were the result of the new people not carrying their share of the expenses. These persons proposed that the remodeling project be stopped until they had the money in the bank to complete the project. The pastor's salary was reduced by five percent, but it would be restored to the full amount if the offerings increased. It was also suggested that since there was more than enough space in the church building that the adult classes be merged.

This true story illustrates that an expanded mission and ministry vision is not always received with enthusiasm. While the factors in this particular situation are more complex than one would expect, we need to face the reality that forces at work in the typical local congregation resist the renewal of the church. In fact, these forces often collide with the desire to see the church be effective in reaching people with the good news of the gospel.

Indeed, most leaders in a congregation will acknowledge that the purpose of the church and the number-one priority is to witness to the saving power of Jesus. In nearly twelve years of counseling with pulpit committees and giving guidance to congregations in the pastoral search process, I have never encountered anyone who disagreed with the idea that evangelism and outreach to lost persons should head the list. Not very many will disagree with the concept that God's vision for the local congregation is that it be a group of persons who are "God's people on mission through ministry." And yet, significant roadblocks thwart actually becoming a company of believers focused on fulfilling the mission and ministry of Jesus.

One of the most formidable barriers, often overlooked and ignored, is what we have termed the "fellowship" of the local congregation. It has to do with the "comfort level" or the "sense of well-being" of persons as they deal with change and the disruption of familiar activities and relationships in the fellowship of the congregation.

However, it may be misleading to use the word "fellowship" to describe this barrier to effective mission and ministry. The biblical word *koinonia*, translated in English as "fellowship," conveys just the opposite of the self-interest we are implying. Rightly understood and interpreted, the biblical word *koinonia* provides support for the mission orientation of the church.

That which was from the beginning, which we have heard, which we have seen with our eyes, which we have looked at and our hands have touched—this we proclaim concerning the Word of life. The life appeared; we have seen it and testify to it, and we proclaim to you the eternal life, which was with the Father and has appeared to us. <u>*We proclaim to you what we have seen and heard, so that you also may have fellowship with us.* And *our fellowship is with the Father and with his Son, Jesus Christ*</u> (1 John 1:1 - 3, NIV). (underlining mine)

In this passage, the drive to share the message of eternal life comes from the first-hand experience of the writer. He has the passion to extend the divine fellowship and the human fellowship to those who have no knowledge of Jesus. This desire to expand the borders of the "fellowship" is most characteristic of *koinonia* (cf. 1:6 - 7).

Moreover, the fellowship becomes a basic component of the mission purpose of the local congregation.

Not only does fellowship contribute to accomplishing the purpose of the church, it is also created by people's commitment to a common purpose. If individuals are dominated by different purposes, they have very little in common and do not develop strong relationships; but people who share a powerful commitment to the same purpose are united by a strong bond.[65]

The fellowship of the congregation, then, should be a strong bond that unites the church and provides a potent motivating factor in accomplishing the mission task. "Fellowship that does not face outward to the tasks Jesus gave His people is less than New Testament *koinonia.*"[66]

Regardless of what ought to be, the fact is that many congregations turn inward and become concerned primarily with their own comfort. One observer of congregational life terms this "koinonitis" or "fellowship inflammation."[67]

> When Christians develop "koinonia" or fellowship to such an exaggerated extent that all their attention and energies are being absorbed by other Christians, evangelistic myopia is likely to settle in. The lost are out there around the church, but they no longer are a high priority. Even when new people come into the church, the fellowship circles have been so rigidly defined that the new people cannot fit it. Strangers are a threat to churches with koinonitis.[68]

The "cure" for this congregational illness is somewhat like the cure for the common cold. Many remedies are available, but the illness persists and often attaches itself to our system when we least expect it. We can deal with the symptoms, but there is no known cure!

One of the ways to deal with this phenomenon in our congregations is to view the opposing forces in categories proposed by Ralph Winter and clarified for our use by Peter Wagner.[69] They have suggested that "modality" (congregational structures) and "sodality" (missionary structures) are fundamentally different. They have radically different reasons for existence and thus operate in ways that are distinct from each other. The basis for the decisions that are made, the focus of their activities and the recipients of their service are separate.

The "modality" term is associated with the congregational structure. It has been compared to the city and municipal structure. It is essentially a "people-oriented" organization. "The basic purpose of the structure is to keep the people in it happy by promoting peace, harmony, and justice."[70] It exists for and promotes the mutual benefits of the residents. One becomes a member of the community simply by moving in.

On the other hand, "sodality" is used to refer to the mission type structures which are more narrowly task-oriented. These are independent organizations which have requirements for belonging to the group and are much more specific in their focus. "The leadership cares much less about the consensus of the opinions of the members than about accomplishing the task for which the organization was established."[71] Examples might be the police department within a city or the Rotary Club.

A contrasting list of characteristics of these two categories reveals their disparity when applied to the local church.

SODALITY	MODALITY
Mission structure	Congregational structure
Task orientation	People orientation
Mission and Outreach	Fellowship and Maintenance
Purpose is focused	Purpose is broad
Governed by vision and purpose	Governed by consensus
Conversion or decision growth	Biological growth
High demand	Low demand
Higher commitment	Lower commitment
Stresses doing	Stresses being
Battleship	Cruise ship

This cursory treatment of this concept is not adequate to explain all aspects of the modality-sodality continuum. It is sufficient, however, to call attention to the destructive polarity which may exist. Congregations must deal with this factor to be engaged in the Great Commission of Jesus.

The word-picture "battleship" to describe the mission oriented church places the emphasis on accomplishing the directive of Jesus to "go into all the world." When a member becomes disgruntled or leaves the fellowship because that member is not satisfied with how he or she are being treated, the "battleship" church does not change course. The captain does not call "time-out" or disengage from the battle to retrieve the sailor washed overboard. The mission is the supreme reason for their existence.

At the other extreme is the word picture "cruise ship." This denotes the purpose for the local congregation as the comfort and pleasure of the passengers. When the passengers are unhappy, every effort is made to satisfy their desires and wishes. If one should fall overboard, the first obligation of the crew is to rescue the person. Great care is given to making all the circumstances pleasant. No cost or effort is too great to satisfy the needs of the fee-paying customers.

The modality-sodality concept does go beyond illustrating the extremes. The real issue is how much of a sodality (with mission orientation) can a congregation become without alienating the very members who give it continuing life and support. Can the congregation (primarily a modality) take on the task of mission outreach without threatening its existence? The answer, of course, is in finding a balance between the people orientation, the modality structure, and the task orientation, the sodality structure.

It is critical that every congregation understand this basic difference in orientation and make decisions that are realistic and yet have a commitment to stretching the capacity of the church to fulfill the mission of Jesus. The continuing questions must be, "How much of our primary energy and resources shall be directed outward toward the spiritual needs of the community?" "How much of our energy and resources shall be focused on our own needs?"

Pastors and leaders in congregations must also recognize that the inclination for all churches is to gradually slide away from the mission orientation to the modality, cruise ship orientation. There is less pain and effort when people are happy and comfortable. "The tendency is for modalities to consume sodalities, or for sodalities to gradually become more and more like modalities in their structure and attitudes."[72]

Another helpful tool for understanding these potentially conflicting forces in congregational life is a chart adapted by John Finney.[73] It is useful to assist leaders in visualizing the task orientation and the people orientation. It is based on a managerial grid which plots a "concern for the task" and a "concern for people."

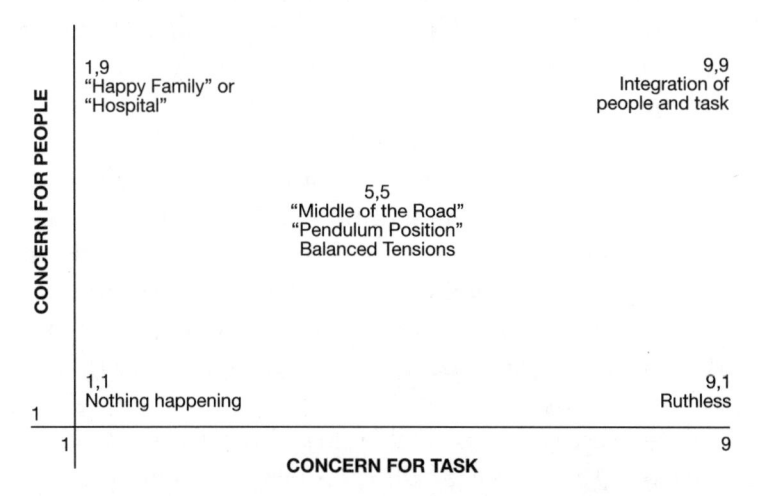

```
                    |  1,9                                    9,9
                    |  "Happy Family" or                      Integration of
  C                 |  "Hospital"                             people and task
  O  F              |
  N  O              |
  C  R              |
  E                 |              5,5
  R  P              |              "Middle of the Road"
  N  E              |              "Pendulum Position"
     O              |              Balanced Tensions
  F  P              |
  O  L              |
  R  E              |
                    |
                    |  1,1                                    9,1
                    |  Nothing happening                      Ruthless
              1     |
                    |_____
                    1                                                9
                                    CONCERN FOR TASK
```

Figure 2. Concern For People and Task Grid

On this grid, the congregation which has a low concern for people and a low concern for the mission task (1,1) is a place where nothing is happening. It neither cares for people nor is it meaningfully engaged in the task. It is either asleep or at ease in Zion.

The church which is plotted at 1,9 is a group greatly concerned with keeping people happy, but not overly worried about the mission task. The leaders often have an oil can ministry which concentrates on keeping any squeaky relationships quiet and running smoothly. They may welcome anyone unless the false warmth and fellowship is threatened. The pastor is usually a "chaplain" attending to the wishes of the people and doing what they want. Any attempt to establish direction for the congregation on the basis of vision or mission purpose is met with fierce resistance.

At the other extreme is the congregation at 9,1. This is the "ruthless" congregation which subverts the needs of people to an overriding concern for the task. It should be pointed out that the task may not be the reaching of the lost. It might be any consuming work which at the same time ignores the needs of people. Indeed, "...all leaders must remember that they can forget and hurt people by an exclusive concentration on the task, even if it is the right one."[74]

The position for optimum effectiveness is plotted at 9,9. This represents the attempt to both achieve God's vision for the church in the mission task and the care of people. The full commitment of the congregation to these dual concerns may at some point bring about a collision of interests in the congregation. However, the empowerment of individuals to accomplish the mission of Christ may in itself be a strong unifying factor.

Fulfillment of the task will in itself care for the needs of many. Their morale is built up as they are helped by the church in their basic mission task. The mutual encouragement, the fellowship and the level of spiritual life increase when something is accomplished together.[75]

The church that is plotted at 5,5 is not so much a "happy medium" congregation as it is a group pushed around by conflicting and shifting positions. Characterized by Finney as being in the "dampened pendulum" position, the church experiences little accomplishment and keeps people only moderately happy. "It has to be recognized that this 'balanced' position, where the conflicting forces in a church are held in a position of tension, is comfortable in theory but in practice difficult and exhausting, and achieves little."[76]

Yes, the vehicles of mission purpose do sometimes collide with the modality structure of the congregation. We must acknowledge that probability! And yet, if the church is to become an effective agent of reconciliation and salvation to those who have not received Christ, then the local congregation must take on some characteristics of the sodality. There must be a concern for the mission task.

My observation is that the loss of vision and mission purpose is a primary reason for congregational decline and ineffective ministry. Recapturing God's vision for the church to be "spiritually alive and engaged in the great commission to go make disciples" may not lessen the potential for problems, but it will move us toward his divine intention.

ENDNOTES

[65] Joe S. Ellis, THE CHURCH ON PURPOSE (Cincinnati, Ohio: Standard Publishing, 1982), 72.

[66] Ibid.

[67] C. Peter Wagner, LEADING YOUR CHURCH TO GROWTH (Ventura, California: Regal Books, 1984), 183.

[68] Ibid., 183, 184.

[69] Ibid., 142.

[70] Ibid., 143.

[71] Ibid., 144.

[72] Ibid., 154.

[73] John Finney, UNDERSTANDING LEADERSHIP (London: Daybreak, 1989), 17, 18.

[74] Ibid., 19.

[75] Ibid., 20, 21.

[76] Ibid.

CHAPTER SEVEN
IDENTIFYING THE OBSTACLES

All too frequently, as I described in the previous chapter, pastors and leaders fresh with enthusiasm and the call of God plunge into ministry only to be surprised and baffled by the response of the local congregation. Many pastors and local leaders, thwarted in carrying out their deep conviction about the mission of the church, succumb to a disillusionment about the church. They sometimes leave the fellowship of believers in discouragement and defeat and become bitter about the future of the church. As someone has commented, "You have to believe in the kingdom to be able to stand the church."

There is wisdom in that saying. First, we do need to have a "kingdom" perspective. It is God's kingdom and he will prevail in this world of sin. The battle has already been won! We are only kingdom ambassadors and we serve the king. Neither the kingdom nor the church is ours. Second, we need to distinguish between God's divine organism, the church, and what takes place in the activities that surround human organizations which may bear the name "church." Every congregation will contain people who have not made a commitment to Jesus Christ as Lord and Savior. They do not all have a personal relationship with God. Some members of the church's organization and active participants in the life of the congregation may have a cultural religion rather than an individual and intimate faith. Other persons may at one time have had a close walk with God but now are only going through the motions. Wise pastors and leaders will be aware of the human dimension that has impact on the mission and ministry of the local congregation.

One of the factors that sends constant reverberations through the life of the church is the speed with which change is occurring in our society. Too often the church has been slow to recognize and respond to changes. Rapid change has rendered many methods ineffective for communicating the gospel to the modern mind. We can't ignore these external pressures on the church by forces at work in our society. They are, in themselves, significant obstacles which pastors and leaders must recognize and manage. The writings of George Barna and Leith Anderson have proved to be a valuable asset to the church in coping with changes in our society. I commend these writers, and others, for serious study of the external influences of change on the local congregation.

The purpose of this chapter is to identify, in broad brush strokes, the internal obstacles which limit the effectiveness of the local congregation in its mission and ministry. I have been a serious observer and a participant in intervention measures in congregational difficulties for more than a decade. I have shared the pain of pastors and leaders and know there exists in some local congregations a wide gap between God's intention and human reality. It is not my purpose to approach the renewal of the local congregation from a negative or problem-solving perspective. However, naming these hindrances will help the church be aware of the opposing forces. Then, with the creativity of the people of God and the guidance of the Holy Spirit, we can find a way to surmount the difficulty.

SIN AND DISOBEDIENCE

Perhaps the most devastating obstacle to effective mission and ministry in the local congregation is the willful and intentional action of leaders who violate God's laws. Not only do they bring condemnation on themselves, but the church suffers agony because its witness is at times nullified. The congregation may be torn within because of violated loyalties and trust. Although the church is in the redemption business, leaders who desecrate their calling and the trust of the body can never fully regain their effectiveness in the local congregation. There may be exceptions, but central to this discussion is the fact that overt sin by leaders destroys and devastates the effectiveness of the church.

Furthermore, it does not take newspaper headlines to damage the church. Hidden sin, though carefully and secretly covered, will eventually bring ruin to the individual and blockage to the ministry of the church. Like the sin of Achan, sin will impede the work of God's people. It will not remain hidden forever. Although the work of the church may appear to prosper, it is clear from the scriptures and the experience of the church that sin and disobedience within the life of the congregation will harm its mission and ministry potential. Unregenerate people placed in positions of responsibility will have a long-term negative effect on the progress of the congregation.

Certainly more subtle and yet more pronounced in practice is the election or appointment of nominal church attenders to places of spiritual leadership. This often occurs because of the low standards of commitment that are expected by some congregations. People who can talk intelligently about the scriptures and matters of theology may without question or examination be given assignments that obstruct the mission of the church. They may be given the authority for decision making which hinders the church in achieving the biblical mandates. The "cultural" religion that they espouse may limit the aggressiveness of the church.

Another type of situation which develops has been named by observers of congregational behavior as "St. John's Syndrome."[77] It is described as afflicting persons who at one time have been fervent in their commitment to God but who now have "forsaken their first love" (Revelation 2:4). Yet, they remain as active participants in the church, sometimes in leadership, and become hindrances to the mission and ministry of the congregation. The focus of this type of person is usually on their personal satisfaction rather than the mission purpose of the church. This trait appears frequently in older congregations where the second generation does not hold the fervent convictions of the parents. The dull routine of religious activity may have replaced the earnest, first-hand personal conversion experience of those who come to faith in Christ.

These and other sin and disobedience-generated obstacles to congregational effectiveness can be discerned from the record of the first century church and subsequent church history. We are warned to "be on your guard" as shepherds of the church of God because persons from outside and from within "will arise and distort the truth in order to draw away disciples after them" (Acts 20:30,31, NIV).

SHALLOW FAITH AND LOSS OF VISION

A whole category of obstacles to the effectiveness of the congregation in mission and ministries can be grouped around shallow faith and loss of vision. These are not necessarily the result of a rebellious attitude toward God and the mission of the church. They may arise out of ignorance, the lack of adequate instruction, or the natural tendency to be protective of what now exists. The resistance to change, in any form, is a part of human nature for many people. We will address that factor when we project strategies for facilitating change in a congregation.

Sadly, many Christians do not see with spiritual eyes the people who are lost and without hope. They have received the blessings of God themselves, but they do not see the persons all about them with the compassion of Jesus. They have cocooned themselves into a protective and satisfying environment and have little desire to jeopardize that sense of satisfaction. They are blissfully unaware of the hurt and chaos that is resident in the lives of their neighbors and co-workers. They may have never been challenged by a larger, potentially upsetting worldview.

We have learned that an aggressive pastor who is concerned about the unsaved and unconverted, the hurting and wounded, is the most important catalyst in awaking the church to the needs of persons. The key to a mission-oriented congregation is a pastor who will take responsibility and pay the price to lead the church to embrace its God-given task.[78] The pastor has a tremendous influence through biblical preaching and teaching and modeling this value in his or her own lifestyle. The corollary is just as true. Should the pastor be unwilling to place an emphasis on the mission and ministry outreach, seldom will the church be effective in mission outreach or service in the community.

Poor leadership, pastoral and lay, may bring about a general weakening of spiritual health in the congregation. Unconcern for the lost and disregard for spiritual fervor may reduce the congregation to a "club" mentality. A selfish, me-centered religion destroys the climate for mission and ministry.

One circumstance that slips up without being recognized has been called "people-blindness."

People-blindness is the malady which prevents us from seeing the important cultural differences that exist between groups of people living in geographical proximity to one another—differences which tend to create barriers to the acceptance of our message.[79]

Congregations may not be aware that their mission and ministry are limited because they are not factoring in the natural differences that are present among people. The church may be "tuned out" by people because they intuitively sense that the church is not really interested in them. Congregational activities may ignore the cultural preference of the very people the church is attempting to reach. While this is an unintentional obstacle, it becomes formidable as the congregation continues to fail to see people as they really are. Contact and interchange becomes less and less as members of this segment of the community pull away.

A very similar barrier occurs when congregations fail to see their physical facilities and certain behavior patterns as an "outsider" would see them. Over time, congregations become accustomed to the appearance of their buildings, how to locate the sanctuary, and where to find class rooms and restrooms. They fail to make their buildings convenient and attractive to the newcomer. Indeed, the people in some congregations are so at home with each other that the friendliness within the group is interpreted as exclusiveness and rejection by the newcomer. Making meeting places and worship services "user friendly" and open to guests is extremely important. The lack of ability to welcome people in a way that is culturally appropriate becomes a significant barrier. Hospitality, personal warmth and friendliness must have a high priority in our congregations.

Lack of faith and loss of vision at times surface in the reluctance of congregations to "pay the price" for expanding and effective ministry. "Doing the Lord's business" is not inexpensive. Ministry is often costly and demands determined faith. The unwillingness to provide adequate worship space, educational facilities or parking leads to "sociological strangulation." That is, when the facilities no longer make it conducive or convenient for people to participate in church activities, they will find other places to go and other ways to use their time.

As we have suggested earlier, the reluctance to adjust fellowship patterns has a chilling effect on welcoming the newcomer. The one-big-happy-family atmosphere can be maintained only until a congregation reaches one hundred in average morning worship attendance. The reluctance to form new groups to assimilate new persons effectively puts a "lid" on the number of people who can become a vital part of the congregation's fellowship. I observe that the most difficult transition for some churches to make is to institute a second morning worship service. This change, by its nature, creates another group. Members feel pain and frustration because "I don't know everyone anymore." That complaint is the sure sign of the reluctance to adjust fellowship patterns even though God is pleased because newcomers often find Christ in the additional service where the space for them has been created.

Other examples of this obstacle appear as the church grapples with the leadership issues. The congregation, to expand the base for ministry, must open the leadership circle. An unwillingness to recruit and train new, untried leaders leads inevitably to stagnation. The church will meet the new challenges of its ministry only if it continually takes the risk of faith that believes that God is now calling people to leadership. The avenues to exercising that leadership must be open and attractive.

In like manner, the pastoral leadership role must not be weighted down with unrealistic expectations. For example, some congregations continue to expect the pastor to relate to persons individually on a one-to-one basis when expanded ministry makes that very unlikely. When a church has grown to nearly two hundred in worship, it will require a different style of leadership than when it was fifty persons. The pastoral needs of the congregation must be met, but expanded ministry always means that other persons will be necessary to share that responsibility. The wise congregation, committed to the Great Commission, will find ways to develop the leadership to meet the increasing demands of ministry.

One additional obstacle seems to be in the path of most congregations. A tendency is to substitute the means of ministry for the "ends" or purpose of their mission and ministry.

Organizations and their leaders deal with two categories of concerns: means and ends. "Ends" are the ultimate objectives, goals, or purposes that an organization is supposed to achieve. "Means" are the tools, the instrumental concerns that help to accomplish the ends. In the church, the God-given ends are evangelizing the lost and restoring the saved to God's design for living.[80]

The reversal of "means" and "ends" is a formidable obstacle. When the "means" of ministry become as sacred and fixed as the "ends" or purpose, then the church becomes mired in unproductive traditions. Preserving the "means" of ministry even though they may no longer be relevant causes the congregation to become fixed in time. Soon the "way we do things around here" is more important than why they are to be done. That opens the door to dull routine, lack of creativity, formalism, traditionalism, and institutional concerns which become the priority.[81] To retain the life and vitality of the church on mission, congregations must keep their purpose central to all that they do. The "means" are always temporary.

THE SINGLE CELL

A special area for consideration in this treatment of the obstacles to increased mission and ministry is the single cell congregation. In recent years we have discovered that the small congregation has a distinctive character to its life and ministry. Carl Dudley and Lyle Schaller have written to enlarge our understanding of the nature of the small church and how it functions. Pastors and leaders of small congregations would increase their ability to fulfill the Great Commission by acquiring a thorough understanding of the single-cell church.

The single-cell congregation is typically made up of sixty to eighty persons who meet regularly for worship. This size of congregation meets the criteria for a primary group, a close knit association of people who have a strong sense of belonging. The family and friendship bonds tend to give the congregation a well-developed sense of security for the individuals included. These persons often have shared experiences that have shaped commonly held values not easily altered. They do have a clear feeling of ownership regarding property, buildings and "my space." While the group size does lend itself to "everybody knowing everything about everybody," real intimacy may not exist. The term "familiar strangers" is an apt description. This type of congregation is very resilient and can withstand external pressures and events which would threaten its existence. However, because it is a primary group, it also resists growth and change very successfully.[82]

An important insight for the pastors and leaders of the small church is to understand that **by its very nature** a small congregation will resist changes that appear to be logical and biblical. The changes that pastors and leaders propose to increase effective ministry will not be opposed because the people are sinful, disobedient, lack faith or have lost their vision. Indeed, the people may be convinced that the changes actually threaten the purpose of the church as they perceive it. Expanded ministry or growth may be a denial of all that the members of that congregation value and hold dear.

First, the strong commitment of the members to one another, to kinfolk ties, to the meeting place, to the concept that the congregation should function as one big family, and the modest emphasis on program tend to reinforce the single-cell character of the small church. When combined with the intergenerational nature of the typical long-established small church, these forces tend to enhance the caring nature of the fellowship, but at the cost of potential numerical growth. These unifying principles tend to make the small church an exclusionary institution. While there usually is not a conscious effort to exclude strangers, these expressions of institutional commitment tend to make it difficult for the small membership church to reach, attract, and assimilate potential new members, unless people have kinfolk in that congregation.[83]

In other words, for the small church to expand its ministry it must be willing to give up the very aspects that give it strength and value. The single cell congregation will not sacrifice those characteristics without a struggle.

Despite the difficulty, the single-cell church can be effective, can change and increase its ministry. We must be aware that the majority of local congregations in North America will fall into this size category. While the estimates in other communions vary, sixty-seven percent of the congregations of the Church of God in Michigan fall into this group. The challenge is to raise the horizons of all congregations so that they are spiritually alive and engaged in the great commission.

The pastors and leaders of small congregations may need to concentrate on what the single cell does best: build fellowship and strengthen individuals. Raising the self-esteem of the small church will be important. Pastors must realize that very likely they will not become the leader. Their role will be to provide the pastoral functions while very slowly and gently walking with lay leaders to new levels of ministry and outreach. Building relationships with existing leaders and developing "allies" who will advise and promote new ministries will be crucial.

COMMON STRUCTURAL BARRIERS

Included in this survey of potential obstacles to the mission and ministry of the local congregation are the natural organizational hurdles almost every congregation encounters as it grows and increases its outreach. These obstacles occur at several points along the path of growth. They are most likely to surface as a congregation needs to make a transition from one method of operation to another. Very often it is associated with the role of the pastor which must change to meet the leadership demands of a new, expanding ministry situation.

One of these structural barriers is, of course, the single cell. When a congregation attempts to move to a multiple-cell structure with several distinct groups and paths to assimilation into the fellowship, a natural resistance takes place. This is usually accompanied by the change from a "family" type church to a congregation which places more emphasis on meeting the needs of a variety of people through multiple programs. Youth ministry, adult and children's choirs as well as children's weeknight activity and training programs open up the avenues for outreach that soon change the character of the church's life. This expands the need for lay leadership for these activities and often brings a tumultuous time as the congregation sorts out its recruiting and leadership-development strategies. Objections to certain new leaders and the tension which results over the distribution of task responsibilities grow out of the natural transition which the congregation is making to a "program orientation."

Another natural structural barrier has been referred to as the "two hundred barrier." This phenomenon has been well-documented in the experience of many congregations. In my tracking of growth statistics for the Church of God in Michigan, I can see clear evidence that many congregations stall near or just over the two hundred mark in worship. This occurs most often when the congregation has been a single cell for a period of time and then begins to grow by using multiple-cell strategies. The growth and expansion of ministry stalls, however, when the expectations of leaders do not match the results. Frequently, leaders continue to think in single-cell terms and are not prepared to deal with the new congregational situation using multiple-cell assumptions.

In addition, while it is possible for one pastor to minister to two-hundred-fifty persons with the recruitment of lay ministers, the capacity of one pastor is usually less than two-hundred persons. The inability of a single pastor to be shepherd of two-hundred persons puts a cap on the growth and ministry of the congregation. The "two-hundred barrier" is a formidable hurdle for any congregation. Not only must the congregation be willing to add the necessary staff for expanded ministry, but the pastor must have the maturity and capacity to give this ministry away. In my experience, not being able to personally be a pastor to all the people and needing "give away ministry" is a difficult transition in role for most pastors.

Lyle Schaller has proposed the following categories as a basis for understanding how congregations may differ on the basis of size.[84] These indicate the natural barriers which congregations and their pastors and leaders must negotiate to progress to the next level.

SIZE	TYPE	ANALOGY
1 - 34	Fellowship	Cat
35 - 100	Small Church	Collie
100 - 175	Middle-sized	Garden
175 - 225	Awkward size	House
225 - 450	Large	Mansion
450 - 700	Huge	Ranch
700 plus	Mini-denomination	Nation

The mere listing of these categories is sufficient to impel pastors and leaders to be aware that while all churches are different, enough similarities within the size categories warrant investigation and research. The barriers to increased mission and ministry should not persist because of the lack of knowledge.

Other persons have identified natural barriers based on the number of pastors and leaders required to meet the pastoral and specialized ministry needs of the congregation. If the personal needs of individuals in the congregation are not met, then difficulties will arise. However, with the commitment of pastors and supportive workers to address the personal spiritual needs of all the people in the congregation, the ministry can surmount the barriers. The different stages of congregational ministry need not become obstacles if the pastoral care of persons is adequate. Staffing for growth rather than maintenance will mean that congregations must anticipate what the next level of their ministry will require and take that step before it is necessary. Again, Lyle Schaller provides us with a beginning point to understand the ratio of full-time staff positions to worship attendance.[85]

Average Worship Attendance	Full-time Program Staff
200	1
300	2
400	3
500	4
600	5
700	6
800	7
900	7 or 8

In other publications, he refers to this same ratio as a plan for staffing to maintain a plateau.[86] The important fact is that the congregation can overcome the natural structural barriers. By the creative recruitment of workers and leaders along with the calling of adequate professional staff, the church can take the next step in fulfilling its mission and ministry without being halted by an unexpected obstacle.

DESTRUCTIVE CONFLICT

The final obstacle which continually seems to block the progress of congregations is destructive conflict. Conflict is a normal part of congregational life. It can be very beneficial and constructive as the church sorts out the priorities and determines what God's plan and purpose is for the local congregation. However, destructive conflict does not build on "kingdom" objectives. It poisons the congregational atmosphere so that persons flee or are driven away by the unpleasantness of the situation. The positive, uplifting and mission orientation of the congregation cannot be maintained very long in the presence of destructive conflict.

One symptom of a growing program of mission and ministry may be the onset of what has been termed the "pioneer-homesteader" conflict. As the congregation attracts new persons the very life of the congregation begins to change. In many situations, the pastor begins to identify with the new persons who take over more and more of the worker and leadership positions. The "pioneers," those who have labored and sacrificed to bring the congregation to its present state, move or are moved to the sidelines. When the newcomers, "homesteaders," reach the approximate number of "pioneers," uncertainty and tension about the future direction of the congregation develops. While there seems to be no single reason for the anxiety, the progress and growth in ministry comes to a halt as the two camps battle over who makes the decisions and who controls the future. Once the battle is engaged, seldom does the church manage the conflict for the "kingdom good." The result is a bitter and divided membership. Stories of personal hurt and offense abound.

While an easy cure for this situation is not possible without radical surgery, it can be avoided. Careful and consistent nurturing of relationships and open communication with "pioneers" is extremely important. Balancing the enthusiasm of new workers with the reliable wisdom of the pioneers in a collaborative style of decision making will build a partnership in ministry. Developing a mission and ministry strategy based on mission purpose, goal setting and strategic planning will minimize the potential for this conflict.

One form of destructive conflict, in my judgment, seems to be on the increase. It is caused by persons, "antagonists," who afflict the church out of their personal psychological or emotional needs.

Antagonists are individuals who, on the basis of nonsubstantive evidence, go out of their way to make insatiable demands, usually attacking the person or performance of others. These attacks are selfish in nature, tearing down rather than building up, and are frequently directed against those in leadership capacity.[87]

Kenneth Haugk, noted pastor, clinical psychologist and founder of the Stephen Ministry approach to lay pastoral care, has detailed this phenomena and gives excellent guidance for leaders and congregations as they deal with it. My own belief is that congregational life cannot be separated from the family systems that have nurtured the people in our churches. Since more evidence exists of dysfunctional family systems in our society today, I believe that these dysfunctional people will be found increasingly in our local congregations. It will be imperative that leaders work together to support each other and give direction for the work of the congregation in a way that does not allow the person with destructive tendencies to impede the work of the church.

This survey of obstacles to a mission orientation within a congregation should not discourage pastors and leaders. It should, however, be a reminder that the path to accomplishing God's vision for the local congregation is neither smooth or uneventful. We must be able to identify the obstacles for what they are: barriers to achieving the full will of God for the church. It will be just as important to have in place methods and strategies which will proactively anticipate the obstacles and prepare the local congregation for negotiating them.

ENDNOTES

[77] C. Peter Wagner, YOUR CHURCH CAN BE HEALTHY (Nashville: Abingdon Press, 1979), 112.

[78] C. Peter Wagner, LEADING YOUR CHURCH TO GROWTH (Ventura, California: Regal Books, 1984), 44.

[79] Ibid., 51.

[80] Joe S. Ellis, THE CHURCH ON PURPOSE (Cincinnati, Ohio: Standard Publishing, 1982), 92.

[81] Ibid., 93.

[82] C. Peter Wagner, unpublished seminar notes (Pasadena, California: Fuller Theological Seminary, August 1986).

[83] Lyle E. Schaller, THE SMALL CHURCH IS DIFFERENT (Nashville: Abingdon, 1982), 53. 54.

[84] Lyle E. Schaller, LOOKING IN THE MIRROR (Nashville: Abingdon Press, 1984), 16.

[85] Lyle E. Schaller, THE MULTIPLE STAFF AND THE LARGER CHURCH (Nashville: Abingdon Press, 1980), 59.

[86] Lyle E. Schaller, GROWING PLANS (Nashville: Abingdon Press, 1983), 115.

[87] Kenneth C. Haugk, ANTAGONISTS IN THE CHURCH (Minneapolis: Augsburg Publishing House, 1988), 25, 26.

CHAPTER EIGHT
AFFIRMING LEADERSHIP FOR THE MISSION OF THE CONGREGATION

Leadership is a hot topic in the world of business and commerce today. Even a quick look at the training seminars and literature currently available reveals concern for the quality of leadership. With the restructuring of business and industry in North America, leadership has become a prime issue. In fact, many persons would say that leadership is the key to the future.

Local congregations are very aware of the need for strong leadership. The most frequent request that I hear from pastoral search committees is that their next pastor be a "strong leader." While that "leadership" is defined in a variety of ways, leadership remains the key. Perhaps the one overriding ingredient that is acknowledged as crucial in the mission and ministry of the local congregation is the quality of the leadership.

In this chapter and the next, I will address various aspects of congregational leadership. I believe that pastoral leadership and lay leadership are complementary and cannot be isolated from each other. Quality in both pastoral and lay leaders is necessary. Pastoral leadership must be recognized as vital to a congregation which is committed to being "God's people on mission through ministry." No less important is the willingness of lay leaders to work with and follow pastoral leadership in ways that are appropriate to the growth of God's kingdom. However, leadership in the context of the local congregation is the primary focus. The concerns of these two chapters grow out of my continuing discourse with pastors and leaders over the past decade.

THE POWER OF BLESSING

I am convinced that many of our congregations are missing the most powerful tools that God has employed in the building of his church. In God's toolbox are many sturdy and effective devices to aid in the ongoing establishment of a congregation. Unfortunately, these tools are often so familiar and so common that as God's artisans we overlook them and fail to take advantage of their ability to make the task less difficult and complicated.

Underlying all the factors that would cause the local congregation to be effective in mission and ministry is a fundamental leadership concept. **Pastors and lay leaders should work together in harmony in the work of the local congregation!**

That concept of teamsmanship is a self-evident truth which finds little resistance and great acceptance. We really do have the expectation that we will be "workers together with God" (1 Corinthians 3:9). The reality, however, is that often we lose sight of that truth in dealing with the routine matters in congregational life. What should be a dual approach to ministry becomes a duel. The tension rises as the stakeholders lay claim to their territory.

Ultimately, the work of the church is hindered and Satan rejoices as the church muddles through the decision-making process and the resulting relationship difficulties that inevitably arise. Fear, suspicion, tension and emotional distance increase among congregation leaders as the effectiveness in mission and ministry declines. Soon the attendance at worship slumps and the difficulty of recruiting volunteer workers signals a problem that no one wants to discuss. The church is in real trouble!

A potent tool in developing relationships for effective ministry is what has been termed "the power of blessing." Some have referred to this as the ministry of encouragement or affirmation. Others have called this "love and acceptance" or "positive regard." I would associate it with "respect" and the "esteem them very highly" phrase found in 1 Thessalonians 5:12,13. In my Church of God heritage, I have heard our older members speak of having confidence in a particular leader.

The kernel of the concept is that a stream of acceptance, love and high regard flows between persons so that the individuals are spiritually affirmed and empowered through the grace of God to become more and achieve more than any thought possible.

In their book, **THE BLESSING**, Gary Smalley and John Trent define a family blessing that provides the ingredients which allow the personal relationship to bloom and grow and become beautiful.[88] This formula for blessing in a relationship is explained against the backdrop of the ancient blessings of the Old Testament literature. They call attention to God's sovereign act in the blessing of Abraham and all the generations to follow. In addition, the personal blessing occurred in the relationships of Isaac, Jacob and Esau. "The blessing," according to these authors, is a means of conveying spiritual resources and hope that become the soil out of which the person grows to become all that God has intended.

A family blessing begins with meaningful touching. It continues with a spoken message of high value, a message that pictures a special future for the individual being blessed, and one that is based on an active commitment to see the blessing come to pass.[89]

Smalley and Trent list five basic parts to the blessing:
• Meaningful Touch
• A Spoken Message
• Attaching "High Value" to the One Being Blessed
• Picturing a Special Future for the One Being Blessed
• An Active Commitment to Fulfill the Blessing

Picture now, if you will, the coming of a new pastor into the life of your congregation. Members express new excitement and new hope for the future. The leaders of the congregation gather at the altar to commission and install the pastor to ministry in your community by the laying on of hands. Does this definition of "the blessing" in any way describe the congregation's activity? What would take place if every leader in the congregation resolved to act on every aspect of the "the blessing." Would we not see the relationships within the congregation dramatically enhanced?

Although the church is not just like a family, there are some striking similarities. Indeed, for individuals to function at their greatest capacity in the area of their spiritual giftedness, there must be a mutual love and acceptance. This is especially important for the pastor and the pastoral family. Certainly the pastor of a congregation must earn and maintain the trust of the people. In my day-to-day experience with pastors and congregations, I have observed that the effectiveness of the pastor is in direct proportion to the level of love, acceptance and regard that flows between the pastor and people.

Of course, just as families are dysfunctional where love and acceptance have been blocked, so churches are dysfunctional for the same reasons. The life and ministry of a congregation can be stifled and stunted simply because the channels of love and acceptance are clogged. Many factors have impact on the effectiveness of a congregation's mission and ministry. Giving "the blessing" to the pastor including a continuing, active commitment to fulfill the blessing is foundational.

As we are learning, dysfunctional families spin a web of control over persons which is activated and maintained by the withholding of approval and the inflicting of abuse. The sad fact is that often this behavior surfaces in the life of a congregation. When it is tolerated and goes uncontested, the church eventually itself becomes dysfunctional. After all, is not the church a hospital for those needing to be made well and whole? The truth that all church leaders need to face is that persons will deal with change, crises and developmental issues in the church in the same way they have handled these matters in their family system. Please understand that I am frankly addressing a very human situation. Let us thank God for his healing and redemptive power which transforms persons into healthy and whole beings.

While the power of blessing should be the dynamism to energize every relationship in the congregation, let me sketch how this concept might apply to the people-to-pastor relationship as Smalley and Trent have suggested.

The people of the congregation through trusted leaders commission the pastor to leadership and ministry through the "laying on of hands." There may also be significant moments of re-commissioning as time passes.

The congregation expresses publicly and personally the value of the pastor and family to the mission of the church.

The people convey their approval, appreciation and confidence in the pastor for their life together.

The congregation shares its hopes and dreams for the congregation by affirming its mission, setting goals, and expressing assurance that the pastor will lead the church into that bright future.

The congregation through its leadership maintains an active commitment to continue the special relationship with the pastor and work together to achieve the hopes and dreams that God inspires.

I believe that every congregation would strengthen its life and ministry by affirming pastoral leadership. Place this concept of "the power of blessing" alongside of the instruction of scripture.

Therefore encourage one another and build each other up, just as in fact you are doing. Now we ask you, brothers, to respect those who work hard among you, who are over you in the Lord and who admonish you. Hold them in highest regard in love because of their work. Live in peace with each other (I Thessalonians 5:11-13).

PASTORAL ADVISORY TEAM

The local church has an ever-present need to develop an ongoing, structural means for enhancing the quality of the relationship between pastor and congregation. Often inadequate communication and feedback have hindered the health and ministry of the local congregation. Many churches have addressed this need by establishing a group of trusted persons to oversee this relationship. The group has been designated by one of several possible titles: Pastor's Advisory Committee, Pastoral Relations Committee, Pastoral Advisory Team, etc.[90]

This strategy is centered in a small group of persons, usually leaders in other positions, who meet regularly with the pastor on an informal basis. The matters discussed by the Advisory Team are shared only within the group. A very high trust level is essential.

The primary function of the group is to serve as a vision casting group and sounding board for the pastor. The pastor shares his or her hopes and dreams for the congregation. The members of the committee act as a support group for the pastor and consider the pastoral care needs of the pastor to be very important.

The group also reflects to the pastor the needs and attitudes of the congregation's members. They endeavor to keep the pastor apprised of the feelings of the congregation on major issues and help the pastor deal with unusual situations.

No votes are taken in this group. It is not a legislative group that decides and then takes action. The purpose of the group is to be a discussion group with the pastor so that the welfare of the congregation and the pastor are addressed in a non-threatening manner.

The pastoral advisory team embodies these concepts:
1. To be a liaison body between pastor and people.

- to alert the pastor to the spiritual climate, moods, feelings and/or issues existing within the life of the church.
- to provide a setting in which the pastor can express concerns to laypersons.
- to be supportive participants in the confrontation of church members in regards to spiritual/moral issues and conflicts.

2. To be a "visionary" group.
   - to brainstorm and dream regarding the future of the church.
   - to provide a setting in which dreams could be shared and discussed as a first step before plans are formulated or implemented.

3. To be a prayer support group.
   - to spend a significant amount of time together praying with and for the pastor, one another and the ministry of the congregation.
   - to act as a support/care group for the pastor.

4. To provide an annual evaluation of pastoral performance.
   - to work together with the Church Council (or major governing board) in completing annual evaluations.
   - to tabulate and process the evaluations with the pastor.
   - to encourage and offer supportive direction to the pastor.
   - to provide accountability for personal and professional growth.

5. To make financial recommendations (optional).
   - to work with the pastor in gaining an understanding of the pastor's financial needs.
   - to provide recommendations to the budget committee regarding salary, benefits, and reimbursements making use of pertinent information (cost of living

index, member's level of income, work load, professional income level of the community, etc.).
- to ensure that funds are allocated regarding any personal development recommendations that the team has made in the evaluation.

The assignment of the pastoral advisory team is broad and intensive. Since the team members have a very pivotal task, their qualifications should be considered carefully. They should:
- be recognized as spiritual leaders within the congregation.
- be growing mature Christians.
- exhibit positive relational skills with congregational members and the pastor.
- possess spiritual gifts of discernment, wisdom, leadership, exhortation, knowledge, prayer, faith or administration.
- be able to understand and express a variety of viewpoints representative of the congregational diversity.
- be committed to and have a reputation for maintaining confidentiality.

The intent of the pastoral advisory team is to facilitate good communication and feedback between the pastor (or pastors) and the people. Promoting harmony in relationships and a unified vision of the mission of the church is extremely important for effective ministry in the local congregation.

The value of this team concept is that it provides for accountability between the pastor and people. The pastor is accountable to the congregation to serve in a manner compatible with the expectations, style and feelings of the majority. The members of the congregation are accountable in that all grievances involving the pastor are directed to an official body designated by the congregation. While members of the congregation may approach the pastor directly regarding matters of concern, the pastoral advisory team has the power to act as an intermediary to resolve difficulties. However, if a member of the congregation does not act in accordance with the established policy and procedure for resolving difficulties, that person must be accountable for such action and must be considered as acting irresponsibly.

Affirming pastoral leadership by providing a means of continuing support and accountability gives not only stability to the relationship between pastor and people, it establishes a base of trust for launching new ministries and monitoring change. The pastoral-team approach has proved to be an effective tool as the local congregation moves from maintenance to mission.

NETWORKING AND MENTORING

A hopeful sign in the affirming of pastors and leaders for the mission task is the reemergence of the openness to networking and mentoring among leaders. The new openness comes, in my view, because pastors and leaders are being severely tested by the complexity of ministry today. They are seeking new ways to respond to the high expectations of congregations and their own unrealistic standards. Burnout is not a figment of someone's imagination. It is real, causing many to withdraw from ministry. There is, however, a fresh awareness that colleagues in ministry can become partners rather than competitors.

It is a reemerging trend because the apprenticeship training of pastors and leaders has strong foundation in the history of the church. The reliance upon college and seminary training has not proved to be the complete answer to the leadership needs of the local congregation. In many communions, the apprentice method of training leaders has been the most practical and effective.

For those now in pastoral leadership, networking with other men and women of like passion and commitment can become the source of great strength for the mission task. As "iron sharpens iron," the supportive relationships and exchange of ideas and concepts can build coalitions of leaders who face together the difficulties of leadership in this era.

In coming years, it will be increasingly important for state and national leaders to develop formal and informal opportunities for pastors and leaders to meet together. Clarifying God's vision for the local church and discovering the means to accomplish that vision will be primary agenda items.

Mentoring takes the networking trend to a more personal and intimate level. It provides a method of support and training, an empowerment for mission, that has promise of filling the wide gaps that exist in the development of leaders for the mission task. The educational track in our colleges and seminaries should be supported and strengthened. However, the rise and acceptance of a personal mentor pattern will enhance the ability of leaders to be effective in mission and ministry.

Mentoring has been defined as

a relational process between mentor, who knows or has experienced something and transfers that something (resources of wisdom, information, experience, confidence insight, relationships, status, etc.) to a mentoree, at an appropriate time and manner, so that it facilitates the development or empowerment.[91]

This definition emphasizes the value of the personal relationship as the vehicle for the exchange between the mentor and mentoree.

What has become apparent in the practice of mentoring is that this relationship can be adapted to fit the needs of the individuals involved. It can be an intensive relationship with the mentor becoming a discipler, spiritual guide or coach. Or it may be a more casual and occasional relationship with the mentor being a counselor, teacher or sponsor. Contemporary and historical personalities do become models for ministry and also have their place in mentoring, but these are less intentional and do not have the same value in building relationships.[92]

The strength of the mentoring concept is not confined to the process of assisting the novice by those with more experience in ministry. An emphasis on peer co-mentoring does provide an avenue for sharing vision, ministry resources, practical methods and personal relationships on a one-to-one basis. It rests on the knowledge that "we really do need each other" in the mission of the church. "A growing leader needs a relational network that embraces mentors, peers, and emerging leaders in order to ensure development and a healthy perspective on his or her life and ministry."[93] Indeed, it is very easy for leaders to become so isolated and frustrated in "doing" ministry that their effectiveness is greatly impaired and they lose the "joy" of their service and walk with God. Peer co-mentoring opens the possibility that leaders can mutually support each other for the good of the "kingdom" as well as their own personal survival.

LEADERSHIP AND MISSION

The mission of the local congregation, however that mission is conceived of or interpreted, is accomplished as leaders fulfill their role and function. There is a positive correlation between leadership and the effective fulfillment of the Great Commission. Competent and constructive leadership is essential to guide the local congregation in the mission task.

The New Testament does include "leadership" as one of the spiritual gifts given to persons to guide the church (Romans 12:8). While we must be careful not to inappropriately ascribe modern leadership concepts to the biblical text, it is apparent that God has gifted certain men and women to lead the fellowship of believers to do his work.

It is also clear that the function of leaders is to lead. A person may be a leader or a follower in different situations and at different times, but it is the role of the leader to lead. It is his or her job to take responsibility for leadership of the group. A leader is one "who guides the activities of others and who himself acts and performs to bring those activities about."[94] This definition highlights the leadership factors of direction, initiative and modeling.

As we have described earlier, the primary function of leadership is to inspire vision and direction for the group. "Leadership is what gives an organization its vision and its ability to translate that vision into reality. Without this translation, a transaction between leaders and followers, there is no organizational heartbeat."[95]

The local congregation has a constant need to be reminded of the central purpose for the church. The vision soon fades or is lost unless this role of leadership is alive. The natural tendency is for the church to turn inward to meet the needs of the existing members rather than focus on the needs in the surrounding community and world.

Leadership is the function of helping people: (1) to realize their common purpose and keep their attention focused on it; (2) to think clearly, act intelligently, and muster resources to achieve their purpose; (3) to work together as a team.[96]

Peter Drucker, noted teacher and consultant in leadership and management, has underscored the crucial role of the leader in achieving the mission.

Non-profit institutions exist for the sake of their mission. They exist to make a difference in society and in the life of the individual. The first task of the leader is to make sure that everybody sees the mission, hears it, lives it. If you lose sight of your mission, you begin to stumble and it shows very fast.[97]

If it is the task of leaders to take responsibility for the vision and mission of the local church and pay the price for guiding the congregation, then the values and behaviors of leaders are important. Modeling these values and behaviors are powerful tools in communicating to the entire congregation what is important. How leaders spend their time and energy goes far beyond what they express in words.

Leaders set examples. The leaders have to live up to the expectations regarding their behavior. No matter that the rest of the organization doesn't do it; the leader represents not only what we are, but, above all, what we know we should be.[98]

Since the example of leaders is so critical to the mission of the local congregation, I have developed a profile for mission oriented leaders. While I would not want this list to be so fixed that it could not be amended by individual leaders, persons who have these attitudes and are doing these things have the mission of the church at the heart of their ministry.

Benchmarks For Identifying Mission Oriented Leaders

Attitudes:

1. Considers the Great Commission as the primary task of the church.
2. Is willing to take responsibility for and provide leadership for the mission growth of the local congregation.
3. Shares ministry with staff and lay leaders.
4. Endorses a ministry which focuses on equipping laity for ministry.
5. Feels comfortable with not being able to directly minister to the needs of everyone in the congregation.
6. Develops a ministry based on vision of the task rather than tradition.
7. Continues to be a growing person and is willing to invest time and money for further training.
8. Encourages and promotes a multiple cell approach to the church's ministry.

Observable Action Steps:

1. Has a fervent prayer life that includes a focus on the spiritual needs of people both inside and outside of the congregation.

2. Spends at least ten percent of the time given to the Lord's work in evangelism or ministry to the unconverted and unchurched.
3. Establishes and monitors their ministry by means of a mission statement and the setting of goals.
4. Incorporates new Christians into the congregation making active leadership roles available to them on the basis of spiritual gifts.
5. Strives to introduce new groups into the life of the congregation which will assimilate new people into the fellowship.
6. Demonstrates concern for the "numbers" and does count the "sheep" as real people for whom Jesus died.
7. Adopts a leadership style that takes the initiative and sets the pace while being attentive to the voice of other leaders.
8. Seeks to lead the congregation to be a place where God is adding to the church those who are being saved.

LEADERSHIP AND STYLE

Affirming leaders in the church as they guide the local congregation in fulfilling the Great Commission is a fundamental and ongoing interaction within the body of believers. Both leaders and followers will need to be in touch with God to catch the divine vision for the local congregation. The dynamic interchange within the local congregation between pastor, leaders and the whole congregation can be marked by mutual support, trust, and enthusiasm for the work of the kingdom. In this positive atmosphere, sharing the responsibility for the mission of the church results in a joyful response to God and each other.

Much of the success in creating this climate for cooperation and joy in ministry within the local congregation comes from the style of leadership employed by leaders. How leaders achieve the vision and mission of the church is crucial. Their personal "style" of communication and interaction with persons within the congregation will, in large measure, determine the outcome.

> *Effectiveness as a leader depends not only on what you do but how you go about it. Some people do the right things (theoretically) but they destroy their own effectiveness by their attitudes, the way they relate to other people, and the strategy they use.*[99]

Since effectiveness as a leader is the target in the mission orientation, leadership style cannot be overlooked. Current secular models of leadership style range along a continuum from the uninvolved leader to the controlling and dictatorial type. These have been identified in ascending order of control: laissez-faire, democratic, collaborative, directive, persuasive and autocratic. It should be noted that situations arise where any one of these styles might be used appropriately for the good of the group.

It is my conviction, however, that leaders in the local congregation should take their leadership style from that which is modeled by men and women of the faith. Without apology, we look to the biblical record for guidance and direction. Certainly the "servant" style of leadership that Jesus taught and lived must be primary. While "servant leadership" has become a popular expression, it is invoked as a concept far more often than it is practiced. Such examples as Abraham, Moses, Joshua, Nehemiah, Esther, Peter, Paul and a host of others become the source and inspiration for our style of leadership.

In addition to the illustrations provided for us in the lives of biblical leaders, the leadership concept found in Ephesians 4:11 - 13 provides basis for the style of pastoral leadership and the method for mobilizing the local congregation for its mission.

> *It was he who gave some to be apostles, some to be prophets, some to be evangelists, and some to be pastors and teachers, to prepare God's people for works of service, so*

> *that the body of Christ may be built up until we all reach unity in the faith and in the knowledge of the Son of God and become mature, attaining to the whole measure of the fullness of Christ* (Ephesians 4:11 - 13, NIV).

The role of the pastor/teacher is that of the "equipper" of persons within the body of Christ. Preparing the people of God for "works of service" to the end that the church is "built up" is the essence of the job description for the pastor/teacher. This new understanding transfers the responsibility for "doing" the ministry to the whole congregation. It does, however, intensify the obligation of the pastor/teacher to be a trainer and equipper of persons for that ministry. The new paradigm for pastoral leadership will in the future move closer to this scriptural style of leadership.

The "equipper" style of pastoral leadership fits very well with the thought that the mission-oriented leader takes responsibility for seeking God's vision for the local congregation's mission and guides the church in fulfilling that mission.

> *An equipper is a leader who actively sets goals for a congregation according to the will of God, obtains goal ownership from the people, and sees that each church member is properly motivated and equipped to do his or her part in accomplishing the goals.*[100]

While the "equipper" model is finding greater acceptance among congregations and there are new attempts to develop that approach to pastoral ministry, a more careful definition of this leadership style will benefit the church. One such interpretation of this style, focuses on the values it provides for the team approach to mission and ministry. It names three possible styles with an analogy to the "inspirer," the "driver," and the "coach."[101]

The "inspirer" style is found primarily in the inspirational leader who could be pictured as being "in front" of people and pulls them along by the strength of the vision or persuasive personality. Winning over the congregation to support the leader's vision and plans is the mode of operation. The leader's communication ability and charisma are key elements in this style of leadership. At times this style may be appropriately utilized, but often there is very little goal ownership by the whole congregation in the long term. Enthusiasm for the leader's goals wanes very quickly.

A second style is characterized by the "driver" who is behind the people and pushes them to reach the goals. This style emphasizes the control aspect as the leader uses the power of influence to drive toward the goal. Conflict is frequently the atmosphere in which this style of leadership operates.

The "coach" style of leader seeks a place alongside of the people and attempts to guide them toward a mutually agreed upon goal. The climate for this style of leadership is collaboration and joint ownership of the vision and goals. A spirit of team work prevails and everyone contributes to the effort just as everyone benefits from achieving the goal.

This "coach" style of leadership is compatible with the "equipper" style portrayed in the Ephesians passage. In the local congregation, this leadership style might be more accurately termed the "player-coach" style. Of course, the persons who employ this style of leadership will seldom remain on the sidelines. A mixture of the "doing" ministry alongside of those who bear the major responsibility will exist for leaders. The entire congregation, properly motivated and equipped, will be engaged in "works of service."

Employing the "player-coach" style of leadership will change the priorities of the pastor/teacher. The "doing" of ministry will be of less importance. Developing other people for their ministry will become the top priority. Six characteristics of effective coaches will radically change the leadership of the pastor of the local church.[102] Coaches:

1. Establish challenging but attainable goals.
2. Recruit members for the team.
3. Inspire the team to maximum performance.

4. Design an effective strategy or game plan.
    a. Maximize strengths.
    b. Exploit opportunities.
5. Conduct team practices.
    a. Develop the skills of individuals and ability of sub-units to work together.
    b. Affirm team players consistently and correct when necessary.
6. Cultivate team spirit in a winning environment.
    a. Value each member's unique contribution to the group.
    b. Applaud individual accomplishment as team accomplishment.
    c. Build group cohesiveness.
    d. Spends time together as a group experiencing both difficult and rewarding times.
    e. Plan regular celebrations.

One factor in leadership has appeared over and over in my consultation with pastors, leaders and congregations. It determines the effectiveness of the leader and the faithfulness of the followers. It is the underlying principle which makes leadership possible or which torpedoes even the most skilled and gifted leader. I call it the "trust factor." Although I will address "trust" later in the context of mobilizing lay workers in the ministry of the local congregation, I consider "trust" as the one factor every pastor and leader must acquire. It is not an option. It is the very essence of leadership. A pastor or lay person cannot lead in team ministry without trust.

Trust is the emotional glue that binds followers and leaders together. The accumulation of trust is a measure of the legitimacy of leadership. It cannot be mandated or purchased; it must be earned. Trust is the basic ingredient of all organizations, the lubrication that maintains the organization, and, as we said earlier, it is as mysterious and elusive a concept as leadership—and as important.[103]

The "trust factor" in the leadership of the congregational leader or pastor means that the church can expect accountability, predictability, and reliability from leaders.[104]

One final issue is important in an understanding of leadership style. Leadership, in its proper definition, is to be distinguished from "management." Although I have not sought to blur the differences between leadership and management, leaders of the local congregation are called upon to do both. Each function is important to the mission and ministry of the church.

Leadership deals specifically with stimulating the vision, influencing the direction for the mission and life of the congregation. Leadership is interested in the effectiveness and purpose of the church. Leadership majors in the faith response to the opportunities before the congregation. Management, on the other hand, is concerned with the mechanics of accomplishing the task. It deals with the allocating of the available resources to achieve the goals. Management handles the practical side of the venture and is interested in the realistic appraisal of the situation and what it will take to reach the desired destination.

"Managers are people who do things right and leaders are people who do the right thing. The difference may be summarized as activities of vision and judgment—effectiveness versus activities of mastering routines—efficiency."[105] While this difference can be overstated, it is important to the mission of the church that both leaders and managers find a common commitment to fulfilling the will of God for the local congregation. If the role of leadership is to spur the church on to envision the possibilities that God has placed before the congregation, then the manager "types" are charged with the responsibility of recruiting, budgeting and planning to reach the agreed upon goals. It is just as important to "count the cost" as it is to "dream the great dreams."

The gift of administration is identified in 1 Corinthians 12:28 and has been associated with the Greek word for

helmsman. The helmsman was the person who had the ability to direct the ship from one place to another and deploy the ship's crew so that the cargo was delivered as it was intended. Thus, a definition of this spiritual gift
is the special ability that God gives to certain members of the Body of Christ to understand clearly the immediate and long-range goals of a particular unit of the body of Christ, and to devise and execute effective plans for the accomplishment of those goals.[106]

It is my conviction that all leaders must be motivated by God's vision for the local congregation's mission and ministry. The team will have individual members who will have certain roles and tasks that will be different, but they will be complementary and mutually supportive. The church is in desperate need of leaders who can "think God's thoughts after him." The church also needs a large cadre of persons who are mobilized according to their spiritual gifts and committed to ministry in the name of Christ. It is to that concern that we now turn.

ENDNOTES

[88] Gary Smalley and John Trent, THE BLESSING (Nashville: Thomas Nelson Publishers, 1986), 24.

[89] Ibid.

[90] The Pastoral Advisor Team concept was developed by the author with the assistance of Dr. Keith Huttenlocker and Pastor Gordon Steinke. A document detailing the program is available from The Church of God in Michigan, 4212 Alpha St., Lansing, Michigan, 48910.

[91] Paul D. Stanley and J. Robert Clinton, CONNECTING (Colorado Springs, Colorado: NavPress, 1992), 40.

[92] Ibid., 41.

[93] Ibid., 159.

[94] Ted W. Engstrom, THE MAKING OF A CHRISTIAN LEADER (Grand Rapids, Michigan: Zondervan Publishing House, 1985), 24.

[95] Warren Bennis and Burt Nanus, LEADERS: THE STRATEGIES FOR TAKING CHARGE (New York: Harper and Row, Publishers, 1985), 20, 21.

[96] Joe S. Ellis, THE CHURCH ON PURPOSE (Cincinnati, Ohio: Standard Publishing, 1982), 142.

[97] Peter F. Drucker, MANAGING THE NONPROFIT ORGANIZATION (New York: Harper Collins Publishers, 1990), 45.

[98] Ibid., 48.

[99] Ellis, 144.

[100] C. Peter Wagner, LEADING YOUR CHURCH TO GROWTH (Ventura, California: Regal Books, 1984), 79.

[101] Conrad Lowe, Pastors' Update Monthly Cassette Program, Vol. 3, No. 10 (Pasadena, California: Charles E. Fuller Institute of Evangelism and Church Growth, July 1992), 1, 4. audio cassette.

[102] Robert E. Logan, BEYOND CHURCH GROWTH (Old Tappan, New Jersey: Fleming H. Revell Co., 1989), 41-51.

[103] Bennis and Nanus, 153.

[104] Ibid., 43.

[105] Ibid., 21.

[106] Wagner, 88, 89.

CHAPTER NINE
HOW TO MOBILIZE A CONGREGATION FOR MINISTRY

Mobilizing people for ministry is the greatest opportunity for the local congregation in this decade. It is also the greatest challenge. The local church should face this dilemma with optimism. The Apostle Paul declared "a wide door for effective service has opened to me and there are many adversaries" (1 Corinthians 16:9, NASB). The real test for the local congregation will be how well it can enlist lay persons in meaningful ministries. Developing ordinary persons into fruitful and fulfilled disciples is the path to realizing the intention of God for the local church as we prepare to enter the next century.

Chapter eight contained a call to the local church to affirm its pastors and leaders for the expanded mission of the local congregation. This chapter is a sequel. Leaders alone cannot do the work of ministry. The task is too overwhelming and the "laborers" are too few. Yet God, in spite of our inability to see his plan, does have a means whereby his vision for the church can be accomplished. It is a partnership between God, pastors and leaders, and the whole people of God. God gives gifts to individuals for ministry. Pastors and leaders affirm, train, guide and coach those gifted for ministry. The entire congregation grows in its capacity to minister to each other and the community as each person accepts and fulfills his or her assignment. These persons grow up "into Christ" because of a commitment to and a sharing in the "body of Christ." Ministry is a natural result of being linked to Christ and to his church.

Biblical concepts strengthen this ministry partnership. The people of God, the laos, is an inclusive term. It incorporates everyone who makes a commitment to be a disciple of Jesus. The laos of God designates every believer regardless of place or assignment within the body of Christ. Those who are ordained to pastoral leadership and called by the local congregation only share the responsibility for the ministry of the church. In addition, when we look at the words in the New Testament for ministry — "serve," "servant," "service" — it is clear that these were not used only of the ministry of the apostles. It was not a ministry reserved for the professional or the elite. Indeed, ministry was the opportunity for everyone to be involved. It was a people's movement.

That concept, however, has changed radically. Today, the common expectation of many congregations is that they will hire the pastor for the work of ministry. It has become the pastor's job to recruit as many helpers as possible to assist in his or her ministry. These are positions to be filled or jobs which must be done if the church is to carry out its program. Very often hostility and rivalry erupts among these persons as they vie for the attention of the church and its resources. Dissatisfaction and burnout from overworked volunteers are problems that occur frequently. Complaints about endless committee meetings with meager support given to the ones doing the work are common. Unfortunately, far more members are consumers than are workers to serve. And the gap widens. Each year it gets more and more difficult to fill the positions of those who resign.

Against that dismal picture is the fresh opportunity that is emerging for the local congregation. This new possibility springs out of the mobilization of people for ministry according to a theology of spiritual gifts. Many churches have found that their congregational life develops a new vitality and that people are eager to be involved.[107] What was once a discouraging and dreaded task becomes more of a logistical problem. Persons want to use their gifts, but where can they find greatest satisfaction? "How and where can I make a difference?" becomes the central question. The congregation often finds spiritual life and renewal as it discovers God's leadership strategy.

A second benefit to the congregation is the improvement in the leadership of the congregation. As the congregation begins to make leadership decisions informed by a theology of spiritual gifts, the quality of leadership tends to improve. The leadership circle is more accessible to the persons gifted by God when spiritual gifts become a primary criterion. Even pastors are considered and called on the basis of their ministry gifts. The result can be a team mobilized to accomplish the work that God has given to the local congregation.

One very important consequence is a new unity that thrives in the relationships of people in the church. The focus turns to a mutually supportive approach to the ministry of the congregation. As people become less defensive about their own "position" and concentrate on sharing ministry according to the distribution of gifts in the body, they become more secure. Often a new openness to innovation surfaces which enhances the sense of freedom in ministry.

When the use of gifts in ministry reinforces the pursuit of the agreed-upon mission goals, this unity strengthens the resolve of the congregation to be on mission for Christ. The "harvest field" becomes greater than the concerns within the fellowship. The church begins to use more of its energy and resources to witness and evangelize its community. It becomes free to "unleash" people for compassionate ministry as it reaches out to its community.

SPIRITUAL GIFTS THEOLOGY

Although my intention is to focus on how pastors and leaders may mobilize the entire congregation for ministry on the basis of spiritual gifts, a brief listing of the biblical concepts provides a substantial foundation. These principles are derived from 1 Corinthians 12 - 14, Romans 12, Ephesians 4, 1 Peter 4 and other passages.

1. Spiritual gifts are God's design.

These passages affirm that God gives special abilities to individuals so that his people will be strengthened and established and his kingdom may grow.

2. God distributes spiritual gifts in his church through the instrument of the Holy Spirit.

It is the ministry of the Holy Spirit to work in the life of the church so that gifts are distributed in a manner that will benefit the work of the kingdom (1 Corinthians 12:4-6, 11).

3. Each person has unique gifts to contribute.

God works in every person to provide gifts that are unique to that individual. No persons are exactly alike, and God gifts persons uniquely. The body of Christ has great diversity (1 Corinthians 7:7, Romans 12:6, 1 Peter 4:10).

4. Each person's gifts are complementary to each other.

In the work of the kingdom, God so gifts his people to bring about a proper "fit" with each other. A gift mix enhances the congregation's ministry. Since gifts are complementary, competition is not necessary. (1 Peter 4:10, 1 Corinthians 12:14 - 27).

5. Spiritual gifts are for the common good.

God's purpose in equipping persons with spiritual gifts is to strengthen the work and ministry of the church. While individuals do benefit from the fulfilling of God's design in their lives, the focus is on the value to the ministry and mission of the church. Mutual advantage prevails as the gifts are shared in the body, but no place exists for elevating an individual gift over the welfare of the community of believers (1 Corinthians 12:7).

6. *There will be adequate distribution of gifts for all the needs of the church.*

If persons will heed the leading of the Holy Spirit and respond appropriately, there will be sufficient gifts present within the body of believers to accomplish what God is calling the local church to be and do. The mission and ministry of the church can be achieved as people allow their gifts to be deployed (1 Corinthians 1:7, Hebrews 2:4).

7. *Spiritual gifts may be dormant and may need to be affirmed by the church.*

It is possible for a variety of reasons that a person may allow his or her gift to go unused or unrecognized. It is of great benefit to the church for leaders and the body of believers to affirm and call upon individuals to discover and use their gifts (1 Timothy 4:14, 2 Timothy 1:6, Romans 1:11).

8. *Every gift is to be exercised in love.*

The context for the use of spiritual gifts in the life of the congregation is love. Without love, the use of spiritual gifts is only a pretext for some lesser motive. Love is the highest value and provides the setting for the effective use of the gifts (1 Corinthians 13:1).

STEPS FOR IMPLEMENTING SPIRITUAL GIFTS

The steps for implementing spiritual gifts in the ministry of the local congregation are very similar to those which have been suggested for individuals. An individual or the church will be mobilized for ministry when spiritual gifts are discerned, discovered, dedicated, deployed and developed.

Discern

The effective mobilization of believers in the congregation for ministry begins with the understanding that spiritual gifts are from God. It is his will and design for the administration of the church and ministry to people. Implementation of the congregation's ministry according to spiritual gifts is not an optional program or method. It is the means by which God has ordained that his work be accomplished.

If spiritual gifts are God's design for the church, then it is important that the local church preach and teach the concepts of spiritual gift theology. The pastor and leaders of the congregation must come to a mutual understanding of the principles which will be taught and lived out in congregational life. Initially, sermons, spiritual gift workshops, leaders' training sessions and teaching in the educational ministry of the church will saturate the church with spiritual gifts theology. The instruction to converts, newcomers and those who come to affiliate with the congregation must be a first order of business. As with all foundational truths, the biblical principles for spiritual gifts can never be assumed or taken for granted. When congregations cease to teach the importance of spiritual gifts and ministry, they will revert to shallow concepts and flawed, selfish behavior.

One of the results of implementing spiritual gifts concepts is that some change may be necessary in the structure of the congregation. Certainly, individuals will need to begin to adjust their personal life and expectations regarding "positions" which have been held as symbols of honor or prestige. The new method will require not only a new way of thinking about ministry, but it will also require different selection procedures. The "majority vote" may not be appropriate in all instances to express the will of God for the selection of leaders and workers. The American democratic voting system may have to give way to a more biblical and spiritual means of selection. Each congregation will need to work through the implications of spiritual gifts for their organization.

Discover

The second step in the mobilization process is to discover the spiritual gifts resident in the body of believers. Teaching the concepts of spiritual gifts is not adequate to fully implement spiritual gifts for ministry. Actually finding out what gifts each person has and how those fit into the life of the congregation is necessary.

Since a number of spiritual gift inventories are now available, the instrument must be selected with care. The personal inventory should be in harmony with the theological stance of the congregation. The inventories do vary widely in how they address such things as the sign gifts and "tongues speaking." Wise pastors and leaders will give close supervision to this phase of the implementation plan.

Spiritual gift workshops and retreats have proven to be very effective for congregations as they seek to discover the gifts of their people. The time away from the everyday distractions in a concentrated period of teaching and discovery has been of great value in this process. Discipleship training and newcomers classes certainly are excellent opportunities to teach people the concepts of spiritual gifts theology and discover how their gifts might be utilized in the life of the congregation.

Leaders in a congregation will also realize that the inventories are just one aspect of the discovery process. Giving people the opportunity to explore various ministries on a trial basis may be very helpful to the individual and also to the ministry. The atmosphere of experimentation for those discovering their gifts will be healthy and productive. Of course, the affirmation of other Christians as people get involved in ministry will help to reinforce their feelings of confidence about their spiritual gifts. Confirmation by the body of believers is necessary in the exercise of the spiritual gifts.

A very crucial facet of the discovery phase will be to devise a means of tracking the spiritual gifts of persons in the congregation. This will be very important for the deploying of people into appropriate ministry situations. Updating this survey of spiritual gifts within the congregation and making it available to ministry leaders, nomination committees and other groups involved in the placement of workers will be an ongoing concern.

Dedicate

One of the strongest statements that a congregation can make to elevate spiritual gifts and mobilize the congregation in ministry is to dedicate people and their gifts before the entire congregation. Commission people to ministry regularly and as often as possible.

The gathering of the congregation to "lay on hands" to commission individuals and groups to ministry becomes a way of highlighting and giving importance to ministry. A congregation will come to honor what pastors and leaders give priority in the life of the congregation. Praying publicly for specific ministry efforts and the people who are involved will give not only added prayer support but magnify the place of ministry in the congregation.

Some congregations have employed unique means of finding persons who are willing to commit themselves to a particular ministry. "Ministry Fairs" have been utilized by congregations to give various ministries an opportunity to tell their story to individuals and provide a means to have persons dedicate themselves to ministry for a limited time.

Deploy

When a congregation moves into this phase, it will need to devise a strategy whereby the spiritual gifts resident in the congregation can be utilized. In this step most congregations fail in the implementation of spiritual gifts. The people may believe in the concept of spiritual gifts. They may be adequately instructed and given opportunity to discover their gifts. There may be the regular dedication of people to ministries of the church. Far too frequently, however, no strategy exists to intentionally link gifted persons with ministries. The missing connection is the placement process.

While ministry according to spiritual gifts has prospered at times in congregations without a workable placement process, the rewards are much greater for the individual and the congregation if a strategy is developed. The informal and unstructured model of spiritual gifts implementation may be the most appropriate form for some congregations. However, if the congregation is able to follow a more intentional course for using the spiritual gifts of believers, the mobilization for ministry will be greatly enhanced.

The writing of job descriptions for each ministry assignment in the congregation is a good beginning place in deploying people. Each job description should include a summary of the job, the duties, time required to fill it, the skills that are necessary and the gifts that are desired. The lines of communication, authority for making decisions and the limits of responsibility should be included. Information regarding length of service and training opportunities will assist people in making their decision. The job description need not be complicated. Simplicity but thoroughness will be appreciated by persons considering each ministry.

Ministry leaders who have a description for each ministry position together with the gift mix of each potential volunteer have powerful resources for the constructive placement of people in ministry. Boards and committees who are often responsible for selection and appointment are better able to match the needs of the ministry and the gifts of persons.

This process is even further strengthened with the enlistment and training of spiritual gift advisors. These are persons who have a thorough knowledge of the spiritual gifts, the needs of the congregation, and an ability to counsel with individuals. They act as the liaison for the various ministries, but are motivated by the desire to see God's will fulfilled in a person who matures and grows in ministry.

The spiritual gift advisor may be the pastor in the small congregation. However, as a congregation increases in size and complexity in ministry, it will become necessary to train other ministers for this task.

Develop

The congregation which is mobilized according to spiritual gifts will initiate an ongoing system of developing the gifts of persons in ministry. The skills and abilities of persons can be honed to increase the effectiveness of the congregation's ministry.

Notice that development follows the deployment phase in this listing of steps. Normally, congregations have thought in terms of discovering the gifts of persons, then developing the gifts of individuals and finally deploying them in ministry. However, the biblical model for the training of leaders seems to be in a different sequence. One author suggests that Jesus followed this process: orient, involve, and equip.[108] A study of Matthew 10, Mark 6:8 - 11, and Luke 10, he proposes, indicates that Jesus called persons from all walks of life to spend time with him. It was not long, however, until they are sent out on a mission. When they return, Jesus uses their experience as a basis for more extensive teaching. They are equipped for greater ministry as they reflect on their experience and the teaching of Jesus.

The methodology that this implies is more like on-the-job training than the model in which a person is trained thoroughly and then deployed for ministry. The "classroom" model of filling the person with knowledge and skills before utilizing him/her has proved to be less effective than we had hoped. Congregations which have trained persons in the classroom for many years continue to have many people "educated" but fewer actually engaged in ministry.

A new form of gift development has appeared in recent years which incorporates this on-the-job methodology. In many congregations which have made ministry a central focus, a regular meeting is scheduled for those involved in the ministries of the congregation. The "ministry teams" encourage one another, pray for one another and learn how to increase their ministry ability. These meetings are powerful in mobilizing persons involved in ministry to greater commitment and effectiveness.

One such leadership development model is called the "V H S" meeting.[109] The letters stand for vision, huddle, skills. The pastor or leader spends a significant amount of time casting the vision and renewing the purpose of the congregation's ministries in the heart and mind of each minister. Then the ministry teams pray together for each other and the needs of the ministry. The session is concluded with a time for skill development.

In addition to being a strong motivation for leaders and workers, this type of meeting in the ministry community provides opportunity for ongoing training. Classroom teaching is added to on-the-job supervision and training. The combination of classroom teaching with mentoring and supervision gives a sound and steady platform for the continuing development of persons and their gifts.

The traditional methods of classroom teaching for concept understanding and knowledge should not be minimized. Many congregations have excelled in the training of persons through this method. However, the in-service training approach seems to be more productive because it combines knowledge and experience. Since the purpose of Christian education is actually aimed at changing behavior, developing the mature person in Christ, it does appear that the "V H S" meeting and other similar in-service methods have great promise for mobilizing persons in ministry.

CONTEMPORARY MODELS

Mobilizing the local congregation for ministry according to spiritual gifts theology is an ideal that is elusive for many congregations. Although a large body of literature currently deals with spiritual gifts, relatively little information explains how that is to be implemented in the life of the local congregation. Theory abounds, but practical examples are scarce. What follows is a summary of several models for implementing spiritual gifts theology. These all, to a greater or lesser degree, mobilize believers in the local congregation for ministry out of commitment to the biblical principles of spiritual gifts theology.

Informal and Unstructured Model

Perhaps the largest number of congregations today who attempt to implement spiritual gifts theology differ very little from the traditional congregation. However, in their structure and mode of operation, they seek to incorporate the concepts of spiritual gifts. They do not change their methods of recruiting and placing persons in ministry positions, but they do change how they view and discuss what is needed for ministry. Spiritual gifts theology and the gifts needed for each ministry inform their decision-making process. I call this the informal and unstructured model.

In this model, the emphasis is upon teaching spiritual gifts theology and helping individuals discover their own spiritual gifts. Through gifts workshops, newcomers classes, and the teaching ministry of the church, a large number of people come to understand the value of spiritual gifts. The principles of spiritual gifts theology are accepted as biblical and leaders acknowledge that these principles need to be incorporated into the life of the church. A listing of people with the various spiritual gifts may be available to ministry leaders and/or committees responsible for appointments and nominations. However, no consistent, structured method exists for placing individuals in ministry according to the criteria of specific spiritual gifts.

One of the strengths of this model is that the placement of people in ministry according to spiritual gifts is a shared responsibility. The entire ministry is formed and sustained by a common understanding. The weakness comes from the reality that time has a way of dimming the vision that was once so apparent to everyone. Soon everybody's business is nobody's business. Appointments and recruiting may quickly revert to filling slots as the fervor for spiritual gifts fades into the background.

Spiritual Gifts Advisor Model

The spiritual gifts advisor model represents a more intentional method of placing persons into ministry positions in the local congregation. One or more spiritual gifts advisors are trained to match the opportunities for ministry with the gifts of persons wishing to make a commitment to ministry. Job descriptions for each ministry are written with the appropriate spiritual gifts listed. The spiritual gifts advisor does need to be familiar with the variety of ministry opportunities in the congregation. A close relationship with the ministry leaders is necessary.

The purpose of the spiritual gifts advisor is to confirm the dominant spiritual gifts of believers and facilitate their placement in ministries where they will be effective and fulfilled. The advisor interviews candidates for ministry after they have completed the spiritual gifts training, discovered their gifts through the inventories, and indicated a desire to be placed. The spiritual gift advisor has in hand at the time of the interview several important pieces of information: the gift inventory, a personal information form, a record of any prior ministry experience, placement forms and a listing of job descriptions for ministries which are indexed by the spiritual gifts needed.

The spiritual gifts advisor and the candidate for ministry discuss the personal desires and the information which has been readied for the interview. On the basis of this interview, the advisor usually gives several options for the candidate to consider. The advisor follows up on the response of the individual and arranges an interview with the leader of the selected ministry.

This is the model which has been promoted by the Charles E. Fuller Institute of Evangelism and Church Growth in the training module for lay mobilization.[110]

Willow Creek Model

Perhaps the most sophisticated and thorough model of spiritual gifts implementation has been developed by Bruce Bugbee, teaching elder at the Willow Creek Community Church, South Barrington, Illinois. In a set of audio tapes and manuals with the title Networking, the mobilization plan for this church is detailed completely.[111]

The strategy for this congregation revolves around an intensive spiritual gifts training seminar for everyone who wishes to become a member of the congregation. Included in the membership requirements of the congregation is a commitment to be involved in some way in the ministry of the church. The intention is to develop "fully devoted" believers in ministry.

In addition to the spiritual gifts inventory, persons are encouraged to consider a ministry on the basis of their temperament, talent and passion. A form of the Myers-Briggs Temperament Analysis is included in the training. Persons are prompted to include any natural talents or hobbies that they have as they survey possible ministry assignments. The program also makes a place for special interests or concerns. These are identified as a particular "passion" that a person may have.

The unique feature of the Willow Creek strategy is that extensive ministry opportunities have been collected in job descriptions which include gift, temperament and passion guidelines. The impressive notebooks contain all of this detail. This model is, without question, the most ambitious in the attempt to mobilize people for ministry.

Skyline Model

A model developed by former Pastor John Maxwell at the Skyline Wesleyan Church, San Diego, California, focuses not so much on the spiritual gifts but upon the practical implications of ministry.[112] The Skyline model recognizes that not everyone has the same gifts, but that everyone should be involved in the Great Commission.

This model is called GRADE: Growth Resulting After Discipleship and Evangelism. It calls for people to commit themselves to one of four positions in a team ministry. The "Abrahams" are those who make a commitment to pray for the entire ministry team. This prayer ministry which has been expanding rapidly at Skyline is noted for being one of the most effective in supporting the pastoral staff and the ministry teams. The "Barnabus" members are the encouragers. They visit shut-ins and are involved in the relational ministries of the church. The "Andrews" are those with the gift of evangelism and are committed to sharing their faith with others. The "Timothys" are people who are involved in the discipling ministry of the congregation.

Although this model does not specifically attempt to implement spiritual gifts theology, it is a very practical strategy which is used in many congregations across the United States.

Bear Valley Model

Reference is made to the Bear Valley Baptist Church, Denver, Colorado, because of the unique influence that this congregation has had on the concept of ministry today. The major contribution that it has made can be explained by the word "unleashing."[113] The ministry of this congregation has grown as its members have become aware of the needs of their community and unleashed the resourcefulness and giftedness of people in the congregation to meet those needs. The emphasis of the congregation has been to have a minimum of structure and a maximum of ministry. The rules and regulations for starting and maintaining a ministry have been kept to only those that are absolutely necessary for accountability. The growth of the congregation has been exceptional. The expansion of its concern into compassionate ministry has become a standard for congregations today. Although the church seems to promote a method characterized as informal and unstructured, it is the nature of its non-structure which makes it a compelling model. The focus of congregational life is upon ministry. It accomplishes the strategy through a radical commitment to have people involved in ministry of their choosing in their own way.

LEADERSHIP FOR MINISTRY

The local congregation is a human resource organization. It is in the "people business." It is more than a cliche' to say that wherever there are people there will also be problems. In my experience with the local congregation, the ministry of the church suffers more from its inability to deal with the "personnel" side of the endeavor than any other aspect. Churches flounder and decline in effective ministry when they are beset by conflict and difficulties arising from the inappropriate relationships between persons in ministry. People tend to shake their heads in disbelief at the powerlessness that occurs when the local congregation does not confront the situation. They prefer to walk away, pretend that the problem does not exist and hope for a better day.

What the local congregation needs is a dynamic leadership able to confront the difficulties, place persons in ministry situations that benefit the kingdom work and fulfill the needs of the individual. This is a leadership that moves the church forward and at the same time empowers individuals for personal ministry. Once again, leadership is a key element in the effective mobilization of the local congregation for ministry.

Since leadership is so crucial, how can the church identify and commission leadership that will take responsibility for guiding the congregation? The vision is to be "God's people on mission through ministry." The local congregation seeks quality leaders who can conduct themselves and the ministry of the church in a manner that would please God and fulfill the divine mission.

In our quest for ministry leaders who would mobilize the church according to God's design, it is important that we turn to the New Testament guidelines for selection. Certainly the directives of Titus and 1 Timothy are appropriate as the church considers qualifications for elders and deacons, and they should be consulted. The qualities of the believer listed in Romans 12 and 13 are desirable and should be growing in the life of every Christian. However, I have come to a great appreciation for the decision regarding ministry leadership illustrated in Acts 6:1 - 7. The guidelines found in this ministry situation can instruct the local congregation in the selection of leaders as it mobilizes for ministry.

The church in Jerusalem was in a dynamic and changing ministry situation. The church was growing and the ministry was expanding. A problem arose, however, among the Grecian Jews who were being neglected in the daily distribution of food. Evidently, those who were not being adequately cared for were vocal enough that it came to the attention of the "Twelve," the Apostles.

Please notice that the difficulty arises from among the believers. As is often the case today, the problem appears from what affects the sense of well-being of the fellowship. It is a predicament which surfaces out of the internal administration of the body of believers rather than out of the evangelistic task.

The response of the "Twelve" was positive, direct and centered on the solution of the difficulty. They were, however, confident and forthright about what they believed God would have them to do in the mission and ministry of the church. In a gathering of all the disciples, they stated their position. "It would not be right for us to neglect the ministry of the word of God in order to wait on tables" (Acts 6:2). It is obvious that while their commitment to the design of God was firm, their priorities were to be different.

The instruction to the believers is specific. "Brothers, choose seven men from among you who are **known to be full of the Spirit and wisdom**. We will turn this responsibility over to them and will give our attention to prayer and the ministry of the word" (Acts 6:3,4). The Twelve identified three criteria for the selection process and pledged their willingness to relinquish the ministry to those whom the group would choose.

When the ministry leaders had been chosen, they presented these to the apostles who commissioned them to ministry by prayer and the laying on of hands. The result was that disciple making increased at a rapid rate. The church grew and its ministry expanded even among the "priests" who "became obedient to the faith" (Acts 6:7).

In addition to the managing of this conflict situation in a manner which led to the expansion of the kingdom, the Twelve identified three components of leadership essential to the local congregation today. These qualities are necessary attributes for ministry leaders as the church mobilizes for its ministry.

Spiritual Leadership Component

The first quality of leadership for the ministry of the local church is the spiritual component. The spirituality of the leader is primary. An intimate, growing personal relationship with God is an absolute necessity. They are to be full of the Spirit. The church must hold up this spiritual qualification as God's expectation for leadership in ministry.

Of course, this spiritual component assumes the regeneration work of the Spirit in the leader's life. There must be a personal faith in God and not just an intellectual knowledge of the truth about God. Being "full of the Spirit" certainly includes the inner condition of being yielded to the indwelling and abiding presence of the Spirit of God. It involves an active commitment to holiness of life provided by the sanctifying action of the Spirit day by day. There should be a growing in the life of the Spirit, constantly maturing in a process that never ends. These are the basics of a life "full of the Spirit."

The spiritual component of leadership can never be taken for granted or treated casually if the local congregation is to be effective in mobilizing the church in ministry. All too often, this component is understated and largely ignored. However, the church which is spiritually alive and engaged in the Great Commission will take the charge of the Twelve as a first responsibility. The church will choose leaders who are "full of the Spirit."

In my judgment, the selection and placement of leaders in ministry according to the gifts of the Spirit is a necessary part of this component. The individual's walk with God and spiritual life are most important. However, to then ignore or refuse to acknowledge the gifts bestowed by the Spirit is an error that the local church may make as it mobilizes for ministry. These individuals, if they are to be leaders according to God's design, must also be willing to be placed in ministry in accordance with the gifts of the Spirit. To deny the work of the Spirit is to be less than "full of the Spirit."

Another evidence of one's spiritual fitness for ministry has to do with the result of the work of the Spirit in the person's life. The Apostle Paul declared that the "fruit" or the "harvest" of the Spirit could be known. "But the fruit of the Spirit is love, joy, peace, patience, kindness, goodness, faithfulness, gentleness and self-control" (Galatians 5:22,23). Every believer, and certainly every leader in ministry, is to be "growing and showing" the increase of the Spirit's work in his or her life. While we must avoid legalism, it is the expectation of God for every disciple.

My study of the work of the Spirit in this verse leads me to believe that to be "full of the Spirit" affects three areas of the leader's life. The first triad (love, joy, peace) are the result of the person's relationship with God. These are displayed in the daily approach to life and become a part of the expression of personality. The second triad (patience, kindness, goodness) describe the work of the Spirit in our relationships with other people. The third triad (faithfulness, gentleness, self-control) are associated with the Spirit's work in the inner person.

In all of these "graces" of the Spirit, we can visualize what God intends for leaders to become. Leaders should be growing because of the Spirit's work in their relationship with God, in their relationships with people and in their own personal inner disciplines.

In whatever way we describe what it means to be "full of the Spirit," it is very clear that it does not mean simply an emotion, sensation or feeling. Rather, it means to be in the life of the Holy Spirit accomplishing God's purposes both in the person's life and for the ministry of the kingdom.

Practical Leadership Component

Those selected for ministry leadership were to be "full of the Spirit and wisdom." The "wisdom" component leads us to consider the practical side of leadership in the local congregation. Leadership, by definition, means working with people. The leaders selected for ministry by the first century church were persons who could apply the revelation, the truth of God, to the everyday experience of people.

The word "wisdom" used in this verse has a rich meaning in both the Old Testament and New Testament. It can mean the very source of wisdom and knowledge in God himself. It is used to refer to the tradition of centuries in the counsel of the ancient fathers and sages. The word may also signify the knowledge that a person gathers in the course of life and living. "Wisdom" can point to the ability to learn the methods, skills and techniques of living which are passed on by instruction and correction.

Out of all the possible meanings of "wisdom," being "full of wisdom" seems to allude to a special ability to understand God's will and how that will applies to human experience. By God's grace and insight through the Holy Spirit, these persons are able to comprehend the design of God and purpose in the plan of redemption and reconciliation. They are then able to communicate or mediate that truth to people in such a way that people respond to God and are helped in the midst of their needs (See Colossians 1:25 - 29).

This component has tremendous implications for leadership in the local church. There must first be insight into God's plan and purposes and then the ability to work with people in such a way that they are able to receive what God has for them. The practical result is that those who receive ministry grow as sons and daughters of God. The emphasis in this leadership component is that people respond positively to the leader and they are helped.

Many times persons with good spiritual qualifications and correct theological concepts lack the ability to work with other people. The selection of leaders for ministry by the local congregation must include the "wisdom" factor. They must be able to demonstrate in practical ways that their leadership and ministry is full of wisdom. They understand the good news, and they work well with people.

Issues such as the appropriate use of spiritual gifts, how persons fit into the overall ministry team, their temperament and personality will be crucial considerations. Certainly the fruitfulness of persons in ministry, their track record, and their effect on other members of the ministry team should be determining factors. The local congregation has the obligation to weigh carefully the "wisdom" or practical component as leaders are placed in ministry.

Relational Leadership Component

Those selected for ministry in the early church were known to be full of the Spirit and wisdom. Other translations say they were "of good reputation." It is quite clear that those chosen were trusted persons of impeccable reputation. They were "brothers" and had proven themselves to the church.

This component addresses the relational aspect of leadership. While these persons were above reproach, I believe that this quality is not so much about morality as it is about their relationship with the church in Jerusalem. These persons were trusted, respected and could be relied upon.

It is also interesting that they had Greek names. It may indicate that they had a natural bond with those they were commissioned to serve. A built-in trust factor was present as they began their ministry. They would be accepted among those who had issued the complaint.

In this relational component, the church must deal with the very human aspect of leadership. No leadership exists without followers. A ministry responsibility must be accompanied by acceptance and confidence from those receiving ministry.

Trust is the key ingredient in this qualification. Trust cannot be demanded or coerced. It is earned over a long period of time as persons prove themselves faithful and reliable. Indeed, service to the body and trust earned in the performance of that service is the biblical approach to leadership and any advancement. Jesus taught that when we are faithful in the small things, we can be entrusted with the larger things, (Matthew 25).

If the focus of the congregation's concern is upon ministry, then the "honor" that is given to persons must reflect the passion for ministry. When the church gives status and prestige, and thus power, to those who hold "positions" rather than to those who serve in ministry, the purpose and mission of congregation is undermined. Yet, at times, the relational component does work against the ministry of the church if it is not balanced with the spiritual and practical components. The church must be careful not to let the desire for "peace and harmony" prevail if persons in "positions" are not actually doing the work of ministry. Sacrificing ministry for good will and tranquility is not the path to being an effective church.

The relational component is a very significant quality for the ministry leader. The leader must have a "servant heart" and be willing to serve according to the gifts granted by the Holy Spirit. These must then be affirmed and recognized by the congregation. "Servant leadership" follows the example of our Lord. The leader must be trusted by the people whom he serves and leads. Ultimately, the leader chosen by the congregation for ministry is accountable both to God and the fellowship of believers.

The local congregation faces unparalleled opportunities for ministry in our day. Regardless of the obstacles and difficulties, the church will go forward if we discover how to mobilize the whole church for mission and ministry. Becoming "God's people on mission through ministry" is the supreme challenge.

ENDNOTES

[107] DISCOVER YOUR GIFTS (Grand Rapids, Michigan: Church Development Resources, 1983), 18.

[108] Robert E. Logan, BEYOND CHURCH GROWTH (Old Tappan, New Jersey: Fleming Revell Co., 1989), 147.

[109] Carl F. George, PREPARE YOUR CHURCH FOR THE FUTURE (Tarrytown, New York: Fleming H. Revell Co., 1991), 134.

[110] LAY MOBILIZATION MANUAL (Pasadena, California: Charles E. Fuller Institute of Evangelism and Church Growth, 1988), 6-25.

[111] Bruce Bugbee, NETWORKING: EQUIPPING THOSE WHO ARE SEEKING TO SERVE (Pasadena, California: The Charles E. Fuller Institute, 1989), audio cassette and manuals.

[112] John E. Maxwell, LAY MINISTRY (Spring Valley, California: Injoy, 1989), seminar on video cassette.

[113] Frank R. Tillapaugh, UNLEASHING THE CHURCH (Ventura, California: Regal Books, 1982), 8.

CHAPTER TEN
COPING WITH CHANGE

Everyone wants progress but no one wants to change. Why? Change is frightening. Renewal, by its nature and definition, means that change will take place. The focus on a biblical mission and ministry will result in the reevaluation of the program of the local congregation. Leaders — guided by the biblical purpose of the church — will consider what the congregations ministry ought to be. Of necessity, there will be a tension between what has taken place, what is now happening, and what leaders propose the church to become in the future. Change, with all of its positive and negative connotations, will certainly be viewed differently by people affected by it.

Change, unfortunately, is not a choice. Everything and everybody experiences change. Change is inevitable! In spite of our desire to avoid or ignore change, nothing stays the same. Every local congregation is in the process of change at this moment whether or not it acknowledges the dynamics that are at work in people and society. The purpose that should direct visionary leaders of the church today is the fundamental belief that the local congregation must be shaped and molded by God's vision for the church. The role of leadership is to understand the forces work in society and the church and guide the local body of believers to be on mission for God through the ministry of Jesus. Like the "men of Issachar, who understood the times and knew what Israel should do" (1 Chronicles 12:32), leaders today must discern God's will in the light of present circumstances to guide the church to fulfill the Great Commission.

CHANGE: PROBLEM AND POSSIBILITY

Wherever and whenever God's redemptive mission has been championed by men and women commissioned by him, change has not occurred without disruption of the status quo. Indeed, men and women under the mandate of God have given sacrificially of themselves to the cause of Christ. It should not surprise us that change is dangerous work even if it is God's agenda. "Christian leaders down the ages have found that proposing and implementing change is hazardous work. They need the necessary skills, bathed in prayer."[114]

Even though the local congregation can be referred to as "God's agent of change" in this world, it is often so caught up in its own ways of "doing ministry" that it becomes resistant to change. The successful "paradigms" of the past become fixed and entrenched so that the church itself becomes a victim of change rather than an agent. The methods that have been fruitful in the history of the church are often retained long past the time they are effective. Because Christians tend to cling to the form of their experiences when they came to faith in Christ and were nurtured into maturity, the church has a tendency to lag behind the contemporary expressions of faith.

We need to be reminded, however, that this natural resistance to change "is good; otherwise they would be like jellyfish, floating with every current. When institutions are unstable, anarchy reigns."[115] The positive side of this reluctance to change is that the local church can provide a solid base for God's people to decide what is the appropriate and effective response to a changing society with the Good News. Wise leaders will resolutely guide the church to be "on mission through ministry" to each generation being careful not to "get stuck" in any single age.

Certain barriers to change in the local church can hamper effective ministry. When these obstacles are dominant in the life of the church, they act as a significant blockage to the fulfillment of God's vision for the local congregation.[116]

1. A Focus on the Organization Rather Than Purpose

When the congregation's energy is consumed by its institutional needs, the mission of the church will not be in the center of its life. God's purpose for the church must be given first priority. When these purposes are known and accepted by the entire congregation, changes necessary to fulfill the mission will become easier to make.

2. Socially Self-perpetuating

There are congregations which find it difficult to accept people who are socially unlike the existing members. While this exclusiveness is often unintentional, it becomes a barrier to change. The small, family-like congregation is very stable but resistant to change when confronted with people of a different background or culture.

3. Minority Rule

Even though we value the democratic approach to decision making, the "one person - one vote" may become an obstacle to change in the local congregation. "Majority rule" soon becomes "minority rule" when the objections of a few dissenters are permitted to control the ministry of the congregation. The desire for unity may overshadow accomplishing God's vision for the church.

4. Yesterday's Innovator

At times, powerful and effective leaders become obstacles to innovation in the congregation's ministry. These may have had outstanding ideas that grew into successful institutional forms of outreach and mission. However, with the passing of years, these persons may continue to insist on doing things as they were in the past. Although the ministry situation has changed, the methods or institution remains fixed in time.

5. Not Inclined to Take Risks

As the local church grows older, it tends to place more value on what it has attained than on the new possibilities before it. The older congregation takes great care to maintain what it has built or created. It becomes more concerned with retaining what it now has rather than risking what it has in order to attain additional goals. The congregation places a high value on stability and becomes conservative in outlook and method.

6. Unwillingness to Suffer Pain

The road of least resistance is not necessarily the best road. Change does mean discomfort and sometimes significant pain. Change affects people in ways that have disagreeable side effects to the status quo. When congregations refuse to face difficult choices with regard to personnel and workers in ministry, the avoiding of confrontation becomes a barrier to change. The unwillingness to pay the price of commitment does hinder congregations.

At the other end of the spectrum is the possibility of change. The local congregation can become what God has intended for the church. The body of believers can seek after and discover the meaning of being "God's people on mission through ministry." For people of faith gifted with an optimism for the future of the church, the best is yet to come. The future of the church is bright and full of potential. For persons with this inclination, change is welcomed and sought after. It is not something to be feared and dreaded, but it is pursued with eagerness tinged with caution and perhaps some anxiety.

The futurist and the catalyst for change delight in dreaming about what God has in store for the church of tomorrow. They challenge the people of God to consider paradigms and structures which do not yet exist. These are the innovators who dare to envision "what might be" by the grace of God. One such "visionary" lists characteristics

he projects for the church of the future as it responds to society's needs.[117]
1. It will be a church which values the personal touch. With the explosion of technology there will be the need for the "high touch" church.
2. The church of the future will provide a wide array of options in serving the needs of people.
3. The coming church will be engaged in sorting the priorities of a new age. It will grow and adapt, but must search for "scriptural filters" to decide how it will respond to the culture.
4. One of the major responsibilities of the church of the future will be to equip people to deal more adequately with the changes in society that are occurring at an astonishing rate.
5. The coming decades will see a change in the way men and women relate to one another. The role of women in the church will be strengthened. Male domination will be altered and the focus on job titles or positions will be changed to emphasize a new partnership in ministry.
6. The church will be more responsive to the "felt needs" of individuals. Addressing the diverse needs of people will be a central emphasis.
7. The organizational structure of the church will be more person centered. Institutional concern will give way to a people concern. Issues will be decided more on how they will affect the person than the structure.
8. The church of the future will need to be more responsive to the desires of the "customer." The leaders of these congregations will be persons who can demonstrate that they care about people. Care giving will be most important regardless of the size of the church.

Change must be regarded by pastors and leaders in the local congregation as both problem and possibility. Change will be hazardous and difficult, and yet there is a new potential to have impact on our world with the message of Jesus Christ. If we take seriously the call of God to be "spiritually alive and engaged in the great commission," the church will be faced with coping with change in the society and in the life of the church.

RECEPTIVITY TO CHANGE

People differ in the way they respond to change. Since persons in the local congregation do have a wide variety of personality styles, it is important for pastors and leaders to acknowledge that these same people will receive new proposals with varying degrees of acceptance. If leaders can understand the inclination of persons toward change, they may be able to avoid the negative or destructive reactions that sometimes occur when new plans and proposals are introduced.

One such study of response to change places people in one of four categories.[118] The continuum ranges from radicals to progressives to conservatives to traditionalists in a decreasing acceptance to change. A description would be as follows.

I. Radicals — Extreme proponent of change
II. Progressives — Proponent of moderate change
III. Conservatives — Supporter of existing conditions
IV. Traditionalist — Opponent of any change

At opposite ends of the spectrum, the radical and the traditionalist are alike in that they operate from an emotional base. They propose and oppose change out of an emotional need to do so. The progressives and the conservatives approach change in a rational manner. They prefer to make decisions regarding change in an intellectual, reasoned manner.

It should be noted that radicals are the source of many good ideas and can serve as the launching pad for new ideas.

However, they may be early starters with a high burnout rate. Since they are by nature in favor of change, any change is appealing to them. Because it is change, it must be better. Unfortunately, radicals are seldom trusted by conservatives and traditionalists and are usually eliminated from the decision making process.

Progressives are often persons who will spearhead new directions for the local congregations. They have attuned themselves to live on the growth edge of life and they are often able to anticipate the next step in the expansion of the congregation's ministry. These people are the risk takers and can become the communicators to the conservatives. They may be the best "salespersons" for any proposed change. They will give energy to the planning process and can be relied upon to go fearlessly into new territory.

The conservatives in the local congregation value things as they are. The status quo is a priority for them. These people are not especially eager to jeopardize their personal comfort. It will be necessary for leaders to be able to justify any change before these persons will accept it. They often ask the hard and penetrating questions and need adequate answers before they are willing to give their approval for a proposal. The conservatives will keep leaders honest in their appraisal of change. They are not risk takers and do demand substantial reasons for making change. It should be said that these people may carry a large portion of the financial burden for the local congregation.

Traditionalists are extremely resistant to change. Since they operate in a very emotional climate, at times they may even be hostile and belligerent. These persons never support change, but they may come to accept it after the new proposal is in place.

One important facet of this analysis is that persons may puzzle pastors and leaders who deal with change. People may be in different categories in different areas of their lives. They may, for instance, be conservative in the work place but a traditionalist in the life of the church. What is critical in this understanding is that pastors and leaders must learn to think of change in the way that others are considering it. Even though leaders may be progressive, they must learn to think as a radical, a conservative or a traditionalist might think. Change affects people! The wise leader will adapt to meet the needs of the people he or she serves.

Another very similar scheme is based on the research of Rogers and Shoemaker who demonstrated that people accept change at different rates.[119] The titles for the categories are instructive and make clear distinctions in the way people accept change. They propose five types of persons in a decreasing scale of acceptance: innovators, early adopters, early majority, late majority and laggards.

Yet another means of classification has helped congregations cope with the tensions that have developed between the long-time members and newcomers. Known affectionately as the "berry bucket theory," it classifies members of the congregation according to two factors. The first is the date of the person's affiliation compared with the arrival of the pastor. The second is the age of that person compared with the age of the pastor.[120] According to Carl George and Robert Logan, the membership of the congregation can be figuratively located in the root cellar on two shelves. There is one shelf for the "formerberries" and one shelf for the "newberries." Of course, the formerberries are the "old guards," long-time members, and the newberries are those who have affiliated with the church since the arrival of the present pastor. On each shelf, then, are two buckets, one for those older than the present pastor, the "seniors," and one for those younger than the pastor, the "juniors."

Although the distribution of the "berries" is not even and varies from congregation to congregation, the impact of change on the four different types is rather predictable. The tenure of the member and the age of the member can give important clues as to how the pastor can work with each group and lead the congregation through the changes in their life together.

A. Junior Newberries (younger/after)	Senior Newberries B. (older/after)
C. Junior Formerberries (younger/before)	Senior Formerberries D. (older/before)

Figure 3. Berry Bucket Theory.

The senior formerberries are the people who have been with the congregation a long time. They have seen pastors come and go, but they have provided support and finances in the tough times as well as the good. They have a strong commitment to the congregation and usually have a strong influence on the life of the church. Even though their numbers may be decreasing, they have given leadership to the congregation in the past and care very deeply about the wellbeing of the church. Often they have married children who also are active in the church. Because these persons had a major voice in calling the present pastor, they will have specific expectations for the pastor based on their past experiences and they are resolute in maintaining these expectations. Frequently, this group is under represented in the worker force of the congregation even though they shoulder a large share of the budget.

The junior formerberries are younger than the pastor and preceded the pastor in their affiliation with the church. Their views of the changes proposed by the pastor will in large measure depend on their relationships with the senior formerberries. Most likely, these people have been raised in the church and may be the children of the senior formerberries. While most of this group will view the pastor and change in a similar manner to the senior formerberries, some will see things quite differently and will look to the pastor for leadership.

The senior newberries are the older members who have come to the church since the new pastor's arrival. For the most part, these persons will be supportive of the pastor if he or she can meet their personal needs. It may be that their affiliation with the church had nothing to do with the attractiveness or competence of the pastor. In such cases, they will tend to be more critical of any proposed changes suggested by the pastor.

The junior newberries are younger than the pastor and started attending the church after the present pastor arrived. They, of all the "berries," will be the most supportive of the pastor's leadership and goals. Very likely, they came to the church because of the influence of the pastor or the pastor's spouse. They quickly identified with the pastor and began to fill the work force openings with their energy and gifts. The formerberries seem to be quite willing to allow these new people to take more and more responsibility.

While there are many implications and instructive insights in this categorization, the purpose for including the "berry bucket theory" is to illustrate that people do respond to pastoral leadership and proposed changes quite differently. It is obvious that the junior newberries are the easiest to lead and respond willing to proposed changes. The senior newberries are often open to change but have mixed expectations for the church based on their prior experiences. While the junior formerberries have mixed reactions to pastoral leadership and change, they represent the next step up in difficulty. Of course, the senior formerberries are very frequently most resistant to change. Incidently, unless the church becomes a multiple-cell congregation, the pastor will never be the leader for this group.

The most significant implication of this scheme is that the pastor and leaders must recognize that this is in reality how many congregations function. Whether we like it or not, leaders must guide the congregation through the maze of these relationships being careful not to upset the delicate balance that would result in open destructive conflict. In my experience, most pioneer - homesteader conflicts can be traced to situations where these relationships were consistently ignored.

Pastors and leaders tend to underestimate the effect of change upon people. One foremost instructor in human behavior has suggested that there are seven dynamics at work when people are asked to do things differently.[121]

1. They will feel awkward, ill-at-ease, and self-conscious when asked to make changes.
2. People think about what they have to give up even while we try to sell them on the benefits. Leaders need to allow people to mourn their loses when change occurs.
3. People will feel alone even if everyone else is going through change as well. There is a great need for sharing and interaction when attempting change.
4. People can handle only so much change. Make sure you prioritize what needs to be done first and do not allow overload to take place. Change should take place over a period of time.
5. People are at different levels of readiness for change. Leaders must be careful not to label people and place them in permanent categories. Be patient and extend a hand to lift them in making change.
6. People will be concerned that they do not have enough resources. They may need help to understand that they have more resources than they realize.
7. If you take the pressure off people, they will revert to the old behavior. Since relapse is natural, leaders should not get angry. Make allowance for relapses, but give a clear picture of what is envisioned and expect change.

THE CHANGE PROCESS

If change can be viewed as a process, perhaps congregational leaders can be more effective in bringing about meaningful change with a minimum of disruption. Understanding the process of change will give wise leaders the informational base upon which to make decisions. When to take the next step and when to wait are crucial in working with people in the local congregation.

Of first importance is the sense of need present in the congregation. Enthusiastically proposing change without a measure of discontent with the present situation is seldom fruitful. In fact, listening to the concerns of people is a key to proposing change. "The amount of discontent with the present dictates the amount and pace of change which can be introduced."[122] As leaders respond to the needs of people in the congregation, changes are more apt to be accepted.

Canon John Finney has suggested that this sense of discontent is a key to understanding when a congregation should move forward in implementing change. He identifies four types of response by persons: the cozy complacent, the restless creative, the frustrated rebellious and the disheartened depressed. These may be placed on a curve to illustrate the management of change.[123]

Level of Discontent

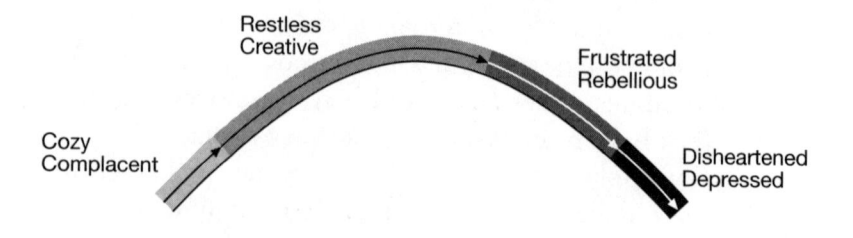

Cozy Complacent — Restless Creative — Frustrated Rebellious — Disheartened Depressed

4. Level of Discontent.

Finney's idea is that as the level of discontent increases so does the possibility of change. However, this is true only to a certain point. If the changes are not made with the proper timing, the situation becomes confused as frustration with leadership sets in and a depression afflicts the church. Timing, then, is all important. The congregation may even divide into two camps as people against change and the people proposing change split over doing nothing.

The process of implementing change follows a consistent pattern and proceeds through steps which can be identified. Joe Ellis provides a very helpful sequence for change in the local church.[124]

1. Unawareness of need.
2. Vague awareness of need.
3. An area of need is identified.
4. Nature of the need becomes clearer.
5. Uncertainty or retrenchment.
6. Rejection, postponement, or foot dragging.
7. Fear and postponement recognized.
8. Commitment.
9. Planning the change.
10. Implementing the change.

Notice that these steps place great stress on the level of discontent as the awareness of need increases. However, in step five and six retreat or uncertainty may take place. To be able to recognize these as legitimate phases that a proposal for change may go through will help leaders to have the patience and tenacity to "work through" these phases.

A leading public pollster, Daniel Yankelovich, has written that public opinion goes through specific stages before it becomes public judgment. While these reflect some of the same dynamics as the Ellis categories, they further illustrate how ideas are processed before they become accepted by the majority of the people involved.[125]

1. People begin to become aware of an issue.
2. They develop a sense of urgency about it.

3. They start to explore choices for dealing with the issue.
4. Resistance to facing costs and trade-offs kicks in, producing wishful thinking.
5. People weigh the pros and cons of alternatives.
6. They take a stand intellectually.
7. They make responsible judgment morally and emotionally.

It is significant to note that in stage four people usually avoid facing realistically the trade-offs that occur in difficult decisions. People often do shy away from making tough choices especially if it affects their comfort and contentment. The need for a clear, defensible mission statement and vision by leaders is a factor in stage six. Without that reasoned approach, the local congregation may never be able to fully embrace stage seven to make significant changes.

STRATEGIES FOR CHANGE

Intentional change does not happen automatically or without great effort. There is a price that leadership must pay to see the local church embrace positive changes that will enhance their mission and ministry. The energy and emotion of people are combined with time and money in the determination to bring about change. Working with leaders over an extended period of time in the context of trust and patient understanding is essential. Too often leaders capture a dream, announce the goals and proceed to pressure the people to fall in step with them to reach the objectives. The processing of ideas and people is extremely important if the whole body is to move together to achieve God's design for the church. Listening carefully to the concerns of people is a prime skill to be cultivated if leaders are to be effective in implementing change.

Leith Anderson has developed a strategy for making change happen in the life of the local congregation. These suggestions grow out of the experience of guiding significant and lasting change in the church setting.[126]

1. Choose to change.

Leaders can take the initiative. Not only is there the opportunity of making a difference, but leaders have the responsibility of choosing among the many options that confront a congregation. They can set the direction and determine the purpose.

2. Persuade the opinion makers.

Wise leaders will concentrate on working with persons who have the ability to influence others. The informal structure and communication lines must not be ignored in bringing about change. Involve persons in the change process who can lead the way and set the pace. Take the time to pre-process the opinion makers.

3. Decide before the decision.

Be careful not to focus only on the stated, formal votes in organizational life that give permission for change. In fact, before any vote is taken on a momentous decision, make sure that leaders are solidly behind the proposal. The vote should be a confirmation of what has already been decided through the informal process.

4. Share experiences to unite people for change.

Any number of shared experiences will bring people together in a united stand on a decision for change. Praying together, sharing in ministry, visiting other sites, going through crisis and participating in group activities are common means of building group solidarity.

5. Raise the predictability of success.

Begin with the concerns and dissatisfactions of people. Insure a good experience by picking a "winner" at the outset. Start small and build ownership in each step by giving plenty of opportunity for input and participation in the process.

6. Encourage and accept accountability.

The leadership of the local congregation will help build confidence and trust as everyone maintains accountability. An annual reevaluation to review purpose and goals throughout the structure will create a climate of mutual responsibility for the mission and ministry of the congregation.

7. *Remember that change can be chaotic.*

Change can be unnerving and upsetting. Leaders, however, will keep their spiritual eyes fixed on the goal of pleasing God through intentional change. Since change is inevitable, leaders should learn to live comfortably with it.

As the leaders of the local congregation anticipate needed change in the life of the church, there are guidelines that will ease the resistance that at times develops. These suggestions arise out of the communication process within the structure of the church.[127]

• Begin with the mission and purpose.

By the emphasis on the mission of the church, leaders elevate the purpose over the means of ministry. The mission of the congregation must be clearly understood and broadly accepted before changes are attempted.

• Communicate clearly.

Using a thorough understanding of the communication process, use every means available to "tell the story." Communication problems often occur because the message received is not always what is intended. Feedback and reinforcement by a variety of communication methods are very important.

• Follow the channels.

Excellent ideas have an unusually short life when leaders fail to follow the proper procedures to gain the support of the church. Think the proposal through very carefully on the basis of adequate information. Process the idea with the opinion makers before taking it to the appropriate committee or authority structure. Make sure that the information reaches all those impacted by the change and that there is opportunity for informal processing before gaining the approval of the congregation.

- Choose the best time and place.

Timing is most important. Avoid the clash of competing agendas and activities. If the change is important, give it sufficient time to mature in the minds and hearts of the people.

- Help motivate for the proposed changes.

Pastors and leaders should take responsibility together for building the climate for the changes to be introduced. The platform of scriptural purpose and effective ministry should underlie the effort. Pilot programs and trial periods are sometimes desirable. Sharing responsibility for the change is crucial.

- Maintain objectivity.

There will be times when the church will need to back up or wait. Rejection of a proposed change may be a signal that all the pieces were not in place. There may be other ways to accomplish the same purpose.

- Follow through.

The formal acceptance of a proposal is just the start. To build the atmosphere for other successful changes in the future, make sure that promises are kept and the follow-through is maintained.

CHANGE AND CONFLICT

There should be no doubt, change will produce conflict. The biblical literature is replete with examples of leaders who faced conflict and in spite of overwhelming difficulties the church prospered and the kingdom expanded. Conflict is inherent in the very nature of the gospel. Leaders in the local congregation must be prepared to manage conflict because there is no escape from it if the church is true to the kingdom message.

However, pastors and leaders must be aware that "our struggle is not against flesh and blood..." (Ephesians 6:12). There is a spiritual warfare that is being waged for the minds and hearts of men and women today. There is the possibility that destructive forces may be at work in the life of the congregation. Kenneth Haugk has written an excellent volume which deals with **Antagonists in the Church**.[128] He gives guidance for dealing with persons who may be destructive in their intent and practice. Although leaders must be very cautious and slow to label any persons as an "antagonist," it is necessary to be realistic about the nature of the spiritual battle.

Nevertheless, I have found that most persons who seem to be in opposition to change have a sincere concern for the work of the kingdom. They are usually people who care deeply about the church. These persons carry in their hearts a love for God and the ministry of the fellowship. Their opposition may spring from one of several reasons.[129]

- Conflict over purposes and goals.
- Conflict over programs and methods.
- Conflict over values and traditions.

It is important to note that there are biblical precedents for each of these motives. The scriptures reveal that conflict can be valuable as the church struggles to understand God's direction for its ministry. The differences between persons in the Bible regarding the fulfilling of the mission of God on earth should make us aware that this will occur in our congregations. Conflict is not sinful, in and of itself. Rather, how we handle conflict and relate to each other in the body of believers is the critical issue.

It is my belief that conflict within a congregation can be healthy if it results in the expansion of the kingdom of God. The church can be strengthened and unified as it "works through" the implications of the Great Commission in its life. Maintaining a respect and value for each other and promoting a style of interaction which gives a priority to "speaking the truth in love" (Ephesians 4:15) will aid the local congregation in fulfilling a God-ordained ministry.

G. Douglass Lewis has developed seven principles which will guide congregations in dealing with healthy conflict.

These will assist leaders in dealing with the human side of conflict and change.

1. *Help others feel better about themselves.*

Persons and organizations manage conflict best when they are feeling good about themselves.

2. *Strive for effective communication.*

Effective communication consists of in-depth and reflective listening and sending with the knowledge that one's perceptions and messages are uniquely one's own.

3. *Examine and filter assumptions.*

Unexamined assumptions contribute to destructive conflict.

4. *Identify goals, what is wanted.*

Identifying what a person, group, or organization is trying to accomplish, what is wanted in a situation is an essential element in conflict management.

5. *Identify the primary issue.*

Until the primary issue has been identified and acknowledged by the principal parties in the conflict, it is difficult to manage the conflict.

6. *Develop alternatives for goal achievement.*

Search for alternatives that will allow all parties to achieve that which is important and fulfilling to them.

7. *Institutionalize conflict management processes.*

To be effective, conflict management processes must be institutionalized and not created solely for special occasions.[130]

In my view, conflict that is processed and managed according to these principles can bring a vitality to the local congregation. When people are important and the mission is central, God is able to so work in the life of people that his will is accomplished for the good of the kingdom.

THE SPIRITUAL DIMENSION

The renewal of the local congregation is first of all a spiritual endeavor. Pastors and leaders should not overlook the spiritual dimension in coping with change. The power of prayer is not limited to the personal concerns of life. Prayer and spiritual renewal can become a primary means by which the local congregation can change the direction of its life and ministry.

> *There is a basic principle in Conflict Management Theory, which says, "During time of organization upheaval, the leader should call the organization back to its norms." That's a complicated way of saying we all need to practice the basics during changing times.*[131]

As human beings, we all want change to some extent. We want change to happen to someone else; we want them to change. Prayer, communion and intercession with God has a way of reordering the priorities. Prayer places the emphasis on "not as I will, but as you will," (Matthew 26:39). When prayer becomes the "glue" that brings people and plans together, the personal agenda and preferences fade in significance. The petition "your kingdom come, your will be done" (Matthew 6:10) has the power to revolutionize the very life of the local congregation.

Prayer does provide a means to empower and unite the congregation in mission and ministry. The congregation which determines to center its life in a renewing relationship with God will increasingly realize kingdom priorities. The will of God does become primary. Prayer can become the avenue by which God leads the congregation to adopt challenging innovations to its ministry.

Prayer also promotes wholeness in the personal relationships within the congregation. It can provide for the healing of wounds and hurts as people resolve to place the welfare of the body above petty personal concerns. The climate of fervent prayer can create a fellowship where acceptance and mutual support make diversity and differences possible. Spiritual growth and the practice of love in relationships can surround the congregation with a confidence where people can risk failure for the cause of Christ.

Wisdom for the spiritual journey and the fulfillment of God's vision for the local congregation can be achieved as we diligently ask God for direction. "If any of you lacks wisdom, he should ask God, who gives generously...," (James 1:5, NIV). The promise for the congregation is that God does grant resources for making decisions about the future and coping with change.

In the last analysis, change "must come as a result of personal spiritual growth of church members, which leads them to an overriding commitment to Christ and frees them to become dynamic participants in the dynamic fellowship of His kingdom."[132]

ENDNOTES

[114] John Finney, UNDERSTANDING LEADERSHIP (London: Daybreak, 1989), 133.

[115] Leith Anderson, DYING FOR CHANGE (Minneapolis, Minnesota: Bethany House Publishers, 1990), 110, 111.

[116] Ibid., 111-118.

[117] Carl F. George, PREPARE YOUR CHURCH FOR THE FUTURE (Tarrytown, New York: Fleming H. Revell Co., 1991), 15-18.

[118] Carl F. George, unpublished seminar notes, "The Change Agent" (Pasadena, California: Fuller Theological Seminary, August 1986), 4.

[119] Finney, 143, 144.

[120] Carl F. George and Robert E. Logan, LEADING AND MANAGING YOUR CHURCH (Old Tappan, New Jersey: Fleming H. Revell Co., 1987), 148.

[121] Ken Blanchard, MANAGING THE JOURNEY: UNDERSTANDING AND IMPLEMENTING CHANGE (Schaumberg, Illinois: Video Publishing House, 1989), video cassette.

[122] Finney, 135.

[123] Ibid., 136, 137.

[124] Joe S. Ellis, THE CHURCH ON PURPOSE (Cincinnati, Ohio: Standard Publishing, 1982), 176, 177.

[125] Daniel Yankelovich, "How Public Opinion Really Works," FORTUNE, 5 October 1992, 102-108.

[126] Anderson, 175-186.

[127] Ellis, 180-189.

[128] Kenneth C. Haugk, ANTAGONISTS IN THE CHURCH (Minneapolis, Minnesota: Augsburg Publishing House, 1988).

[129] Norman Shawchuck, HOW TO MANAGE CONFLICT IN THE CHURCH, Vol.1 (Indianapolis, Indiana: Spiritual Growth Resources, 1983), 11.

[130] Douglass G. Lewis, RESOLVING CHURCH CONFLICTS (San Francisco: Harper and Row, Publishers, 1981), 49-69.

[131] Leith Anderson, A CHURCH FOR THE 21ST CENTURY (Minneapolis, Minnesota: Bethany House Publishers, 1992), 242.

[132] Ellis, 181.

CHAPTER ELEVEN
A PLAN FOR RENEWAL AND VISION

God has begun his reviving and revitalizing work among pastors and leaders. Congregations are catching a new fervor prompted by the Spirit of God to be the church God wants them to be. There is an active longing to be empowered and motivated by God's vision for the mission and ministry of the local congregation.

In the past we have referred to this dynamic of the moving of God among his people as the "revival" or, more currently, "renewal" of the church. Today, the word often used with this energizing of the church is "vision." The church will be renewed when it grasps God's vision for the people of God. Renewal involves an understanding of and a determined commitment to the design that God has for the individual disciple and his will for the body of believers.

If our intent is to capture God's vision for the church, to be spiritually alive and to go "make disciples," how is that attained? What is required of leaders? What demands are placed on the local congregation? Just how do we go about pursuing that "vision"? In other words, what are the steps on this road to renewal?

In this chapter, I want to develop a plan for renewal and vision for the congregation which is truly serious about being GOD'S PEOPLE ON MISSION THROUGH MINISTRY. Becoming a church that is effective in its mission and ministry to the world will not just happen. We cannot fall haphazardly into doing what is pleasing to God. Only by intentionally, patiently, fervently seeking to "be" God's people and "do" his work will the church catch God's vision and be renewed according to his design.

STEP ONE – PERSONAL COMMITMENT

The first step on the road to renewal of the church is the personal commitment of leaders. Those persons who are charged by God and commissioned by the believers to look after the well-being of the body bear the weight of obligation to lead the church into being God's people and doing his will. If leadership can be discerned as taking responsibility and paying the price, then leaders who waffle in accepting their assignment fail God and the church. Spiritually lukewarm leaders are just as distasteful to present day disciples as they are to God. Those running away from the tough tasks lose the commendation of God: "Well done good and faithful servant" (Matthew 25:21).

A careful, prayerfully considered and personally responsible preparation for renewal will include these fundamental elements:

1. Assess Your Spiritual Life

This calls for a brutal honesty before God. Just how is it between you and God? Are you comfortable in his company? At what level are you in your relationship with the Lord? What would be the next step to make a significant difference?

2. Determine to Maintain the Spiritual Battle

Often we forget that God brings spiritual health and victory through the very basic avenues of his grace to us: prayer, Bible study, devotional reading, listening to God's prompting. The spiritual battle will be fought day by day in the trenches of ordinary occurrences. Be sure to keep in mind the importance of physical and emotional health. Leaders cannot run their engines at full throttle if the gas tank is empty. The physical, emotional and spiritual threads of our lives are so intertwined that a break in one puts strain on the others.

3. Expectantly Ask for God's Vision for Your Future

There is no substitute for spending time with God! Prayer and listening in his presence can go beyond the "minimum daily requirement." The yearning for the fulfillment of God's will in your personal life will become more than a perfunctory prayer or a passing wish.

4. Set Aside Time for a Personal Retreat

The purpose of this time alone with God is to zero in on God's design for your future. Pursue God's vision for your personal ministry and family life. "What is it that God wants me to do with my life?" Actually write out a personal mission statement with specific goals which capture this vision. Valuable guides can give you direction in a two or three-day spiritual journey. Many camps and retreat centers offer inexpensive facilities for this crucial yet exhilarating exercise. Remember, maintaining your vision over a long period of time will require vigilance and tenacity. Even the most vibrant, sparkling image of the future will fade if it is not refreshed periodically. While changes may take place, the confidence that God is giving you direction will give energy and purpose for your ministry.

5. Share Your Vision with Trusted Leaders

In this stage, it is necessary to become vulnerable to the community of believers. Seek out persons of prayer who demonstrate spiritual power and maturity. Seek and accept their counsel and advice. Be sure to be true to what God has given you!

6. Adjust Your Priorities for Ministry

When you have a clear understanding of what God is calling you to be and do, begin to reorient your time and energy expenditures into these avenues. However, don't forget the advice of trusted leaders. Allow the perceived needs of the fellowship to temper the desire for swift or cataclysmic change. Leaders will need to ask serious questions.

"What is really important?" "What is not a priority for me?" "What is it that only I can do in this situation?" "What can I give away and at the same time help someone else find his or her place in God's work?"

7. Develop Ministry Allies

The renewal of the church will not take place in isolation or with "lone ranger" leaders. Find those who share your vision and passion for the future of the church. Cultivate a network of people who long for God to reenergize the church. Walk with those who will help you discover the implications of personal renewal and discipleship. Begin by recruiting prayer intercessors who will covenant to be prayer partners with you. All persons, especially leaders, need to be accountable to another individual or group for their spiritual health and vision for ministry. Look for a Barnabas who can encourage and guide you in the difficult times when your vision dims or strength wanes. Form partnerships with persons who will challenge and sharpen your vision. Stay close to God and keep vital friendships to give you the spiritual energy for ministry.

STEP TWO – PURSUE GOD'S VISION FOR MISSION AND MINISTRY IN THE LOCAL CONGREGATION

Without question, God uses individual men and women whom he calls to lead his people to renewal and effective ministry. God has always utilized individuals who were spiritually attuned to his work and his way. However, God's mission in the world has been accomplished when his people have responded to the prophetic voice crying in the wilderness "prepare the way for the Lord" (Matthew 3:3).

The prophet was important in the plan of God, but the goal was to bring the whole body, the nation Israel or the church, to the place where they were faithful representatives of God in the world. Even though they have been passive, apathetic and discouraged, God has reenergized his people when they have taken the step of faith to follow their leaders in pursing God's vision for the church's mission and ministry.

I want to suggest several components which will form a strategy for this second phase of a plan for establishing a new vision and bringing renewal to the church.

1. Teach and Preach the Biblical Purpose of the Church

In addition to the personal commitment to and fervent prayer for the renewal of the church, persistent sharing of the biblical mandate of the church is essential. Effective preaching and teaching on the basic themes of the saving and redeeming activity of God will have contemporary meaning for the church as well as provide historical and biblical foundation.

Dialogue among the believers must take place if the church is to be relevant to the issues of our day, not a relic of time. Consistent teaching which draws the disciples of today to consider the timeless message of salvation and reconciliation will of necessity lead to timely application of the truth. Tough questions must be asked. "What does it mean for our congregation to be on mission for God and engaged in the ministry of Jesus?"

Discipleship classes, special studies, sermon series and small dialogue groups which focus on the purpose of the church constrain the local congregation to take a fresh look at the priorities.

2. Get the Facts Together

Now is the time to do your homework. Chart the course of the congregation for at least the past twenty-five years. Through worship attendance records, Sunday School enrollment, financial stewardship journals, the history of pastoral and lay leadership, and the chronicle of the congregation's events and significant achievements draft a picture of the church's recent past. Be charitable, but be accurate.

Then make a survey of the congregation's present ministry. Who are the people now being served? What ages, life situations and patterns are apparent? Are there gaps and obvious deviations from the general population demographics of your community?

Where is the energy for ministry now being expended in the life of the congregation? By calculating the hours necessary for preparation and the actual amount of time given by pastoral staff and lay leadership engaged in each ministry position, determine the emphasis of the congregation. How much of this ministry is focused inward on the needs of present members? How much is directed to those outside of the church into the community? How many workers actually take ministry responsibility and how does that number compare with the number of people who attend worship? In other words, what is the ratio of "workers" to "consumers"?

3. Seek God's Timing for Change

Redirecting the energy and emphasis of a congregation's life toward intentional ministry and evangelism will take patience and a determination to wait on God's timing. That may begin with an honest assessment regarding the ability of a congregation to make the necessary changes.

The attempt to be "God's People on Mission Through Ministry" will force every congregation out of its comfort zone. However, to coerce the leaders of a congregation to make radical changes is to invite disaster in relationships and ministry effectiveness. Premature or involuntary changes even though considered by some to be essential may result in destructive conflict and the fracturing of fellowship. Although total consensus may never be possible, care must be taken so that leaders move together in concert for any new ministry directions.

It should be noted, however, that some dissatisfaction and unrest is necessary before new directions can be implemented. Seeking God's timing for change will take into consideration human readiness factors as well as the inner pressure to fulfill the call of God.

4. Establish Mission Purpose

The leaders of a congregation can give clarity to the purpose of a local church by developing a mission statement. In both broad and specific language, a mission purpose focuses the efforts and energies of a congregation toward an agreed-upon aim. A common understanding of what "this" congregation is to achieve for God has the power to give definition and direction to the life and ministry of the church.

There are many ways to establish a mission purpose, but leaders meeting together in a retreat atmosphere gives opportunity for the building of relationships while dialogue takes place. The unity of purpose that comes from this endeavor gives great strength to the local church.

5. Develop a Shared Vision for the Congregation

Although leaders should have a vision for their personal ministry, a vision for the local church should be produced by pastors and leaders. After extensive dialogue and exploration into the will of God for the church, a shared vision begins to emerge which is specific and detailed. The mission purpose becomes fleshed out in definite goals and plans to reach those goals.

A significant aspect of this phase is the conviction that God's will is becoming evident in the life of the congregation. This is more than just a goal-setting process or the routine planning of future events. The pastor and leaders develop a confidence that God is revealing his plan for the congregation. This shared belief gives tremendous energy and motivation to accomplish what God is calling the church to do.

A shared vision must then be communicated to the whole body of believers. At every opportunity leaders "cast" the vision so that it becomes common to the language and thought of the entire congregation. It is the vision of doing God's will together for the "kingdom good" that brings unity and cohesiveness to the body of believers. Renewal is at hand.

STEP THREE - MOBILIZE FOR CONTINUING EFFECTIVENESS: GOAL SETTING AND PLANNING

The danger that lurks in the shadows for every church that begins to experience renewal in its life and mission is the dimming of the vision. People do tend to grow weary in "well doing." The constant drain of time and energy depletion is a fact that leaders and congregations must face. Although the leaders in a church have a personal and corporate commitment to renewal in the church, the vision will not be sustained without continuing attention.

Even though the details of the vision may be accepted by congregational members, the implementation will take place over a long period of time. Mobilizing a congregation for effective ministry for the long term requires a strategy establishing a direction for congregational ministry, a proposed destination and mile markers for the journey.

Unfortunately, many congregations falter after the momentary spurt of enthusiasm that follows a "mountain-top" experience. Step three of this plan is a method to initiate an ongoing, intentional means to effective mission and ministry for the local congregation. It assumes a personal commitment to renewal by leaders in the congregation. It also assumes that a shared "vision" for the mission and ministry of the church has, at least, begun to emerge.

1. Gather Leaders for Assessment

In a setting which is conducive to prayerful and concentrated thinking, gather the leaders for an assessment of present and future congregational mission and ministry. The agenda is surprisingly simple. Someone has said that

high-priced and sought-after organizational consultants ask only three basic questions:
   a. Where have we been?
   b. Where are we now?
   c. Where do we want to go?

With that elementary agenda, begin with the strengths of the congregation's ministry. "What has been successful in our life and ministry together?" "What have been the most positive experiences of the past year?" After setting an affirming atmosphere, move to the harder issues. "What are our challenges?" "What are our most significant obstacles to effective mission and ministry?"

Remember, the process may be as important as the product. This shared experience by the leadership team will provide a strong footing for building unity and consensus for implementing God's vision for the congregation. Developing relationships and sharing personal values are extremely important in the phase. Above all, make this event spiritually enriching for each person.

2. Visualize the Future Through Faith

The leaders of the congregation are challenged to go beyond the present realities to envision the future. "What is God calling us to 'be' and 'do' together?" "What is God's intention for us?" These questions probe the purpose and present vision for the church's mission and ministry.

A very stimulating exercise for leaders would be to answer these questions. "If we could do anything in our community and knew we would not fail, what new ministry would please God?" "If we had all the money we needed and all the gifted people necessary, what would God ask us to accomplish?"

3. Discover the Power of Setting Goals

One of the most powerful things that the people of God can do for the ministry of the church is to learn to walk by faith. The corporate demonstration of faith in God and the future of the church is expressed in the setting of goals for mission and ministry. I believe that God moves congregations beyond wishful thinking and good intentions through a commitment to goal setting. Important to this process is an agreement by leaders that goals are statements of faith which propel the church toward God's vision. Worthy goals which are attainable will be a stimulus for the congregation to move forward. Every goal should be specific enough to know when the church can celebrate the accomplishment.

4. Set Short-Range Goals

There are some things that a church could modify easily and quickly with very little effort and cost. This is the place to begin. Immediate improvements will encourage those responsible to take action and set the stage for greater expectations. Creating an atmosphere of hope and positive advancement is vital to the long-term progress of the church.

5. Establish Long-Range Goals

Five- and ten-year goals are essential to the fleshing out of God's vision for the church. Based on a thorough understanding of the needs of the community, the gifts and abilities of the people presently in team ministry along with those whom God will supply, project the faith goals for future mission and ministry. Rally the entire congregation to embrace these worthy, attainable and measurable targets.

6. Determine the Intermediate Steps

The check points along the way to long-range goals are very helpful in gauging progress. Intermediate-range goals may be able to give the indication that "We really are going to achieve our goals!" A sense of confidence and increased trust will develop as leaders are able to demonstrate that the congregation is making progress toward a larger and more difficult goal. Often priorities become an issue. Certain decisions and achievements must be made before others can be attempted.

7. *Make the Planning and Implementing Process Circular*
One of the indispensable factors in the renewal of the church is that the vision casting and faith goal setting be a continuing feature of life of the congregation. It cannot be done once and then laid aside as if it were set in concrete. It would be very unlikely that the vision could be achieved even if no changes or alteration were ever made. People and situations change continuously! The church must have the ability to adjust and redeploy its resources to meet the challenges that God gives to it along the way. The following elements, if included in an annual never-ending circular process, can guide the congregation to achieve God's purposes:
   a. Keep the mission purpose before every decision-making group.
   b. Restate the vision of the congregation.
   c. Set new goals in alignment with the purpose and vision.
   d. Plan to meet goals.
   e. Take action to implement goals.
   f. Evaluate progress toward the goals.
   g. Make any correction necessary.
   h. Reestablish the purpose and vision.

Conviction concerning God's vision for the church, faith demonstrated in established goals, rigorous self-evaluation and faithful commitment to the task are components in the renewal of the church.

STEP FOUR – AGREE ON THE MEANS OF MINISTRY

One of the very crucial steps to renewal of the local congregation and effectiveness in ministry is to come to a working agreement on the means of ministry. The methods used by the local congregation to accomplish its ministry becomes extremely important. Since pastors and leaders approach the tasks of ministry with varied backgrounds and specific expectations, it is essential that a local congregation decide how ministry will be performed. While the consensus may never include every individual in the church, there must be sufficient agreement on the methods employed by leaders to move the congregation toward the goals it has established. One of the sad facts of congregational life is that conflict and confusion often dominate the atmosphere of the church when this issue is not faced and resolved. The tension of opposing opinions and the destructive undermining of the efforts of leaders by well-meaning people can bring the progress of a congregation to a halt. The work of the Spirit and the mission of the church become buried in the avalanche of problems that roll over the congregation continually.

The following represent the issues that must be resolved in this step of a plan for renewal. It should become apparent that this step involves a highly individualized process for each congregation. Every local congregation must itself work through this step if it is to become effective in its mission and ministry.

1. Admit That Your Congregation Has Personality

No two congregations are exactly alike. While that may seem obvious, congregations often pretend they are not unique. They avoid thinking through the issues and coming to agreement on their distinctiveness. George Hunter wrote, "Every congregation has a personality. Whether written or not, each church has a philosophy of ministry."[133] Each congregation has great diversity. The unity of the church is not determined by uniformity in the means of ministry but by the common purpose of the Great Commission.

Accept that your congregation is different and that God's vision for your mission and ministry will be different from every other congregation. Congregations must discover what their particular mission is and how God would have them to accomplish their ministry.

2. Determine the Focus of the Congregation's Ministry

This issue deals with the objective of the congregation's ministry. "Who are you trying to reach?" The typical but unreasonable answer is "Everyone!" No congregation can reach "everyone." To assume that stance is to fail in mission and ministry. No congregation can devise a ministry which will evangelize and disciple every person. Since your congregation has unique people with unique gifts, unique temperaments, unique interests, unique backgrounds, unique concerns, it follows that your congregation will be able to minister through personal relationships that arise out of this uniqueness.

Asking such questions as "Who has God prepared us to reach?" will be the essence of this issue. Although targeting is a concept taken from the world of marketing, it applies to the local church. The means of ministry adopted by the congregation should fit the culture of the people the congregation is trying to reach.

3. Decide on the Style of Music and Worship

No other congregational issue has greater power to unite or divide than the style of its music and worship. Since persons tend to preserve and protect what brought them to faith in Christ, music and worship styles often become a battleground. Pleasing "everyone" in the congregation becomes a preoccupation of leaders. The emotional and cultural side of this issue is overlooked by people when they insist that the music and worship be "just like it used to be." On the other hand, music and worship should lead the congregation to express praise and devotion to God in ways that are meaningful and inspiring. Preferences and cultural background will always be an issue as a congregation decides its course.

What is essential for an expanding ministry is the use of music and worship forms which are "culturally relevant" to the congregation's mission community. Leaders must be concerned about how effectively the forms convey the "good news" to people outside of the fellowship to the "target" community. If cultural barriers exist, then the congregation will not be able to fulfill the mission of Christ in its community. There must be enough relevance in the forms of worship to be attractive so that those outside are not repelled by the "language" barrier. A balance, however, between the mission objective and the personal needs of present members will be a major concern.

4. Clarify Specific Ministry Values

Very prominent in the life of every congregation are ministry values which guide the mission and ministry of the congregation. If these are left to chance and happenstance, they will become a hindrance to ministry because of the expectations of people in the congregation. These values need to be clarified, articulated and supported by the leaders and congregation for a harmonious and unified team ministry. As these issues are examined and decisions are made, the ability of the congregation to move forward with strength will be greatly increased. However, if they are ignored so that tensions and divergent opinions pull individuals in different directions, then the power of the congregation for ministry is diminished. Among these issues are the following:

- The style of evangelism. How will persons be confronted with the gospel? What is the strategy for winning people to Christ?
- The spiritual gifts to be used. What will be the place of spiritual gifts in the congregation? What biblical gifts are recognized? How will the use of gifts be subject to the whole body?
- The style of leadership. What leadership style is appropriate for the congregation and what is not?
- The preaching style. Is there a preaching style which communicates to the people and the community better than others?

- Community involvement. How will the congregation carry on ministry in the community? What compassionate ministries are needed by people and can be provided by the congregation?

5. *Establish a Design for Fellowship and Nurture*

Establishing a design for the ongoing life of the congregation will be essential. The place of discipleship training and nurture becomes increasingly important as the mission and ministry of congregation expands. The role of the Sunday church school in this scheme must be decided. The structure of small groups to guide and to assist in the assimilation and discipling of new persons must be addressed. How will persons be welcomed and find their place in the body of believers? Will there be a means to assess the needs of persons in the congregation and how will that be monitored? How will the pastoral care of persons be accomplished by the congregation? A host of similar questions highlight the need for a thoughtful and intentional procedure for addressing the fellowship and nurture aspects of congregational life.

6. *Structure a Means of Governance*

Every congregation will have a means of governance which is based on its polity and view of organizational life. Since many methods can accomplish the purposes of the congregation, it is necessary to structure a way to guide the corporate life which is accepted and supported. Such things as legal incorporation, bylaws, lines of responsibility and authority for decision making can give direction and strength for ministry. They can also hinder and impede the progress of the church if they are not carefully reviewed periodically. How a congregation will deal with a proposed change often surfaces as problems arise. A means for conflict management must be spelled out. The calling of pastoral staff along with the choosing and placement of leaders become critical issues and should be decided before the crisis arrives. These corporate matters are not insignificant. When addressed with a concern for the renewal of the church, bureaucracy and historical inflexibility can be modified so as to open the avenues for ministry and service to people.

7. Establish Relationships with All Christians

The local congregation can include in its means for ministry an alliance with all believers everywhere. Rather than being isolated and alone, the church can be united in cooperative relationships and ministry. The local congregation has the opportunity to determine the level at which it will share ministry in its community, state, and nation. Since the local church has a global responsibility, the cooperative relationships with other Christians can greatly strengthen the mission perspective. Commitments and accountability to state and national structures should be clear and not based on personal preferences. Appropriate financial support for the total mission of the church should be agreed upon and given prominence in the budget of the congregation. United in prayer and common concern for the needs of people, these relationships will reach across denominational boundaries for compassionate ministry in every community.

Agreeing on the means of ministry cannot be ignored without serious impairment to the renewal of the local congregation. Continuing effective ministry will be achieved as these issues are faced courageously in the spirit of Christ. The following suggestions can assist the congregation to achieve a working consensus:

1. Develop a mutual understanding on each of these issues by intentional dialogue among pastors, leaders and congregation. Keep at it until there is widespread support and agreement.
2. Write out the position which is agreed upon. Communicate this in as many ways as possible. Teach newcomers as they affiliate with the church.
3. The means of ministry will develop over a period of time. Try not to attempt too much definition all at

once. Give adequate time for understanding and consensus to develop.
4. Be tolerant of those who disagree, but be firm when a working consensus has been achieved.
5. Keep the means of ministry as stable as possible without constantly changing the strategy.
6. Be willing to promote change when it is really needed. Follow the recommendations for coping with change.
7. If there is a repeated pattern of conflict over a means of ministry, carefully consider the possibility that God may be calling some members to establish another congregation to reach another group of people.

God is calling the local congregation to be "God's people on mission through ministry." The renewal of the church can be accomplished by God's grace and our willingness to do what is necessary to allow him to work. The steps to renewal open the way for God to give the local congregation his vision for effective mission and ministry.

ENDNOTES

[133] George G. Hunter, YOUR CHURCH HAS PERSONALITY (Nashville: Abingdon Press, 1985), 26.

CHAPTER TWELVE
ANTICIPATING THE HARVEST

Anticipation! We either savor it or we dread it! Whatever is ahead for us, if we have some notion of the consequences, causes us to eagerly long for the time to quickly arrive or seek some way to delay it. We relish the idea of the coming experience or we try to avoid the reality.

Imagination and anticipation can be blessing or curse. Our response really depends on our estimation of how the future event will impact us. We can either be pessimists or optimists when we handle the uncertainties of the future.

Indeed, most of our present-day advertising builds on the tendency to picture our future with eager anticipation or some frightful imagination. Seldom do we buy goods and services on the merits of the product. Rather, we often make purchases because of imagined or anticipated outcomes that we project into the future.

The central thrust for my message to the local congregation is that God has prepared for the church a future that it has not yet captured or anticipated. God has a design and plan for the local congregation which is more fruitful and effective than has been dreamed possible. It is the dawn, not dusk, for the church. God is leading the local congregation to a fresh and more challenging mission and ministry as we approach the twenty-first century. He is calling the church to be "God's people on mission through ministry." It is the challenge to recapture God's vision for the church to be spiritually alive and engaged in the Great Commission to "go make disciples."

The concept of the "harvest" in scripture is an agricultural metaphor which refers to the anticipated ingathering that will take place in the future. In some places, "harvest" is a distant possibility associated with the "end times." In others, however, the "harvest" is of immediate and pressing concern. It carries the urgency of the present-day matters which demand attention.

With this sense of gravity Jesus anticipated the "harvest." *Jesus went through all the towns and villages, teaching in their synagogues, preaching the good news of the kingdom and healing every disease and sickness. When he saw the crowds, he had compassion on them, because they were harassed and helpless, like sheep without a shepherd. Then he said to his disciples, "The harvest is plentiful but the workers are few. Ask the Lord of the harvest, therefore, to send out workers into his harvest field"* (Matthew 9:35 -38).

The context for this event is an on-the-job "leadership training" experience for Jesus' disciples. The Master is on a Galilean ministry trip. He has been teaching in the synagogues of the district, preaching the message of the kingdom and making people whole through his healing ministry. Evidently, he is dismayed by the distress of the people who throng to him. Jesus is deeply moved and experiences deep pain because of his love for those who are without a guide in their confused and defenseless situation. They are powerless to find a remedy. They are lost and without hope. They have no leader.

Jesus addresses these persons he is about to name as disciples and send out with specific instructions. "The harvest is plentiful but the workers are few. Ask the Lord of the harvest, therefore, to send out workers into his harvest field" (Matthew 9:37b-38). Jesus anticipated a bountiful harvest. The abundance of the fields were not in question. The shortfall came in the number of workers available for the task. Jesus knew that there was going to be a problem with the outcome if the "Lord of the harvest" could not send "farm hands" into the fields. The strategy for the anticipated plentiful harvest was simple and straight forward: petition for more laborers who can bring in the harvest.

The words of the Lord are most appropriate for the local congregation of today. Indeed, a bountiful harvest for the mission and ministry of the church can be anticipated. The people whom God loves and calls are all about us, but they are "harassed" in life and "helpless" without hope in God. The "harvest" is ready and urgently in need of attention. The solution, as in Jesus' instruction, is to pray for the increase of workers to serve in the mission and ministry of the church according to the vision of God for the local congregation. Four elements constitute a strategy for anticipating the "harvest."

PRAYER

The first element for anticipating an abundant harvest is prayer. Although prayer is neither novel nor new in the history of the church's mission, it has become neglected in many local congregations. While all forms of prayer are beneficial for spiritual growth, intercessory prayer is the most available resource for strengthening the mission and ministry of the church. One observer of congregational life has said that "intercession of Christian leaders is the most under-utilized source of spiritual power today."[134]

If the local congregation is to realize the full potential of the harvest in its mission and ministry, the effort must begin with a commitment to pray. Even though pastors and leaders have at their disposal vast amounts of knowledge regarding effective ministry today, prayer is the primary resource.

Those who depend on the power of the flesh will be limited to the power of the flesh, while those who depend on the power of the Spirit will never find a limit! Prayer is God's method for linking the efforts of His people with the power of His Spirit. If all Christians would give prayer a top priority — refusing to begin any activity until it is undergirded with earnest prayer — the work of the kingdom would leap ahead. Every great revival has been first of all a prayer meeting. Remember, prayer is the energy that powers the kingdom.![135]

This declaration brings to mind a real and physical encounter in the Old Testament literature which was resolved by spiritual means. In the story of the Exodus, the nation of Israel meets the people of Amalek in battle in the valley of Rephidim. Joshua is the general leading the troops. Moses is on the hilltop overlooking the battlefield and beseeching God on behalf of their general and warriors. Following orders, Joshua engages the Amalekites in battle. Moses soon discovers that as long as he holds up his hands the Israelites prevail. As he tires and lowers his hands, however, the battle goes against them. The battle is won only when a stone is placed under Moses to sit upon and Aaron and Hur stand on each side to hold up his hands "so that his hands remained steady till sunset" (Exodus 17:12).

This incredible occurrence is an example of the teamwork and support that is needed among leaders in a local congregation. God will bless our efforts as we share the load and responsibility for the task. Tremendous spiritual power and victory is available to the church when it prevails in prayer for those who are engaged in the battle. Without question, "The prayer of a righteous man is powerful and effective" (James 5:16).

My concern for pastors and leaders engaged in mission and ministry is that they are deeply involved in the struggle with evil. Yet, they are often without the most effective resource available to them. If we take seriously the biblical concept of "spiritual warfare," a sinister dimension is added. The more successful we are in claiming the territory of the evil one, the more liable we are to his attack. Spiritual victories can only be sustained by the presence and power of God. We can "plug into" that power for those on the battlefield through intercessory prayer.

Intercessory prayer is that "effective," "fervent," "powerful" prayer on behalf of another who is engaged in God's kingdom work. It is a deeper level of prayer that intercedes with God, "your kingdom come, your will be done" (Matthew 6:10) in the life and ministry of the Christian leader or pastor. While every Christian should learn the richness of the close walk with God in prayer, we have in our congregations persons who can become "prayer warriors" to intercede on behalf of those engaged in ministry. Frankly, that is where I believe the battle will be won.

Let me suggest four biblical truths as you think about prayer and its relationship to our mission and ministry.

- Prayer is a scriptural mandate.

Before the New Testament church could be effective in witness and proclamation they "tarried" in prayer until they were filled with the power of the Spirit. The biblical record is full of examples of those who prayed for God's intervention in their situation. Even Jesus was disappointed in his disciples who failed in the most crucial time, "Could you men not keep watch with me for one hour?" (Matthew 26:40). There is a clear precedent in the record for our present mission.

- Prayer is necessary for protection from evil.

The Bible assumes the opposition of Satan. We are given many admonitions to be on guard, to "take heed," to be wary of the onslaught of the evil one who is determined to defeat the cause of God. He is the "thief" who "comes only to steal and kill and destroy" (John 10:10). As I have viewed the victories and the tragedies of men and women engaged in ministry, I have come to believe that prayer for those in the front-line ministries is essential.

- Prayer is required for spiritual victory.

Spiritual victory is neither accidental nor easy nor automatic. There is a price to pay. Intercessory prayer may be a price that someone is paying even when we do not know that it is taking place. The Apostle Paul wrote to the church at Colosse sending the greetings of Epaphras and this note: "He is always wrestling in prayer for you, that you may stand firm in all the will of God, mature and fully assured. I vouch for him that he is working hard for you..." (Colossians 4:12,13). To the Roman church Paul wrote, "I urge you...to join me in my struggle by praying to God for me" (Romans 15:30). Our faithfulness in prayer for pastors and leaders is certainly a key to spiritual victory in our churches.

- Prayer is the foundation for the proclamation of the "good news."

The "gospel" is the "power of God for the salvation of everyone who believes" (Romans 1:16). That is basic to our understanding of the dynamics of the message. That communication, however, takes place through human means. Once again, Paul was very conscious that prayer was a crucial part of the strategy. "Pray also for me, that whenever I open my mouth, words may be given me so that I will fearlessly make known the mystery of the gospel.... Pray that I may declare it fearlessly, as I should" (Ephesians 6:19,20). The battle may be won in the prayer room more often than in the pulpit.

VISION

God's vision for the mission and ministry of the local congregation was perfectly modeled by Jesus as he encountered those who came seeking him. Notice how Jesus responded to the situation with spiritual eyes of vision and faith.

- Jesus was acutely aware of the ministry situation.

Jesus was immersed in teaching, preaching and healing. It must have been demanding and exhausting both physically and spiritually to meet the needs of people. And yet, he was able to look beyond those who pressed in around him to see the larger picture. He saw the crowds. He knew what was taking place around him even as he was engaged in personal ministry to people. Like the "men of Issachar who understood the times" (1 Chronicles 12:32), Jesus was aware of the climate of his surroundings. When he saw the crowds, his vision included an awareness of the circumstances which caused their helpless condition. The context of ministry, with all of its ramifications and complexity, was in the mind of the Master.

- Jesus saw the needs of real people.

This vision was of real people with real needs. These were persons to whom he was sent "to seek and to save" (Luke 19:10). He identified with their hurts and difficulties. Jesus saw them as harassed and helpless and in need of a shepherd. They were individuals, persons with unique and special longings. Each had exceptional potential as a son or daughter of God.

- Jesus responded with compassion.

The Master was moved by the plight of persons he encountered. He became personally involved, untiringly giving of himself to persons in hands-on ministry. He was not a distant, aloof leader with a philosophical belief in ministry. He wept and mourned over the human tragedy about him.

- Jesus saw what people could become.

He was able to see the end result when God was allowed to work in the lives of people. Jesus saw people in the light of what they could become. He saw them as sheep following the true shepherd. He saw them whole persons redeemed by the loving kindness and power of God.

- Jesus saw what needed to be done.

His vision was specific. More workers in the harvest field was the answer. The yield was ready and bountiful. What was needed was an adequate number of workers placed in the fields and actively engaged in the harvest.

- Jesus saw how the task would be accomplished.

Included in his vision were men and women who would be commissioned and sent out by the Lord of the harvest to complete the task. Ordinary people, just like the men he was teaching and training, would be called and entrusted with the mission. As the Father had sent him, so he would send men and women to complete and fulfill his mission and ministry.

The local congregation must capture a vision of its mission and ministry as did Jesus. Without a vision the church wanders from its purpose. Vision for mission and ministry will give direction and meaning to life of the local congregation.

FAITH

If the local congregation is to anticipate the harvest through God's blessing, then faith will be a central fact of its life. In the words of scripture, "without faith it is impossible to please God" (Hebrews 11:6, NIV). Faith is not an optional addition to the life of the local congregation. It is woven into the very fabric of every believer's relationship with God and into the very purpose of the church.

There are many uses of this word faith in the New Testament which encompass a host of meanings. None of the meanings for faith has more significance for the mission and ministry of the local congregation than confidence that God will work within his people so as to accomplish his will through them. "...being confident of this, that he who began a good work in you will carry it on to completion until the day of Christ Jesus" (Philippians 1:6, NIV).

While faith begins with a knowledge of God and the assurance of a saving relationship in Jesus, it is expressed in the action of persons who are filled with hope and expectation for the future. This hope is demonstrated in positive faith statements about the open doors of opportunity. Faith envisions the future and prepares for the fulfillment of the plan of God. Like the patriarchs of the Old Testament period, the church must view its destiny as under divine providence. God's plan will be accomplished regardless of our human failure and limitations. "By faith Abraham, when called to go to a place he would later receive as his inheritance, obeyed and went, even though he did not know where he was going" (Hebrews 11:8).

Faith includes the certainty that what does not now exist can come into being by the power of God. If God gives realistic faith based on the promises of his Word, then our plans and priorities will reflect that potential. "Now faith is being sure of what we hope for and certain of what we do not see" (Hebrews 11:1, NIV). God is limitless; that is faith. However, we do have limitations, so we must establish priorities.

The benediction of Paul on the church at Ephesus becomes the watchword of faith.

Now to him who is able to do immeasurably more than all we ask or imagine, according to his power that is at work within us, to him be glory in the church and in Christ Jesus throughout all generations, forever and ever! (Ephesians 3:20).

The local church will become infused with this attitude if faith is at work.

OBEDIENCE

Just as individuals must respond in obedience to the call and command of God, so also the local congregation must be obedient to the demands of corporate discipleship.

If we want to be his disciples, we must accept his supreme authority as Lord over every part of our life, without exception. If we are not willing for him to be our Lord, he cannot be our Savior. With Jesus it is all, or nothing. To be in the kingdom of God is to accept Jesus as King; and if he is King, his word has final authority and must be obeyed.[136]

As harsh and exacting as this may seem to be to modern public opinion, the directives for the church are as binding as they were for the first disciples. The anticipation of the harvest as envisioned by Jesus includes willing followers who demonstrate their discipleship with a faith that becomes action.

Obedience leaves no room for half-hearted commitment or aimlessness for the local congregation. Although every congregation will have individuals who are at different levels of discipleship and who may view the task of the church in various ways, the purpose must remain constant. The local congregation is to fulfill the mission and ministry of Christ. The specific vision will be shaped by an infinite number of human and contextual factors in the life of the congregation. Yet, the mission mandates of Jesus must be the guiding and overriding concern for the church.

When the local congregation centers its life on anticipating the harvest, it will respond joyfully to the challenge of its mission and ministry. Several activities will naturally flow out of this stance.

- Mission and ministry vision.

The congregation will view ministry through the eyes of Jesus. With this vision of the harvest, they will have the ability to see the needs of people and the strategies for accomplishing the task.

- Commitment to obey.

The church will say "yes" to God in the Great Commission to "go make disciples." The focal point of its life will go beyond maintaining the present status to embrace a mission orientation. Balancing the needs of present members with a strategy to reach the uncommitted, the congregation will live out the call of God in its corporate life.

- Ministry through spiritual gifts.

The congregation will deploy for ministry according to God's spiritual gifts to members. The spiritual power for ministry will be channeled by the Holy Spirit through leaders and workers. This partnership with God and each other causes the church to grow and be firmly established in Christ.

- Faithfulness to the task.

Faith becomes faithfulness in ministry. Obedience results in a tenacity that overcomes the emotional highs and lows that accompany working with people. The local congregation will develop a stubborn determination to translate the words of faith into deeds of love and service.

INCREASING ANTICIPATION FOR THE HARVEST

When these four elements interact and build upon each other in the life of the local congregation, the anticipation and expectation for the harvest increase. Prayer is the initial element because only through this close, intimate relationship with God can the church begin to understand the will and purpose of God in the world. This dawning understanding leads to a vision of the lost through the eyes of Jesus and a vision of how the church should be engaged in the mission and ministry of Jesus. Faith, a belief in the possibility of what God can do through his people, is engendered in the hearts of devoted disciples. Faith grows and is tested in obedience as the church launches out and becomes engaged in the work of the kingdom. God blesses the "harvesters" with increase as men and women are brought into the kingdom by redeeming grace. The church is forced to deeper prayer for God's guidance and blessing as they continue to experience the response of people to the "good news" of the kingdom. What takes place is an ever-increasing spiral of effective mission and ministry in the name of Jesus. Anticipating the harvest means that the local congregation is willing to allow God to fulfill the mission and ministry of Jesus in its life.

Harvest Circle

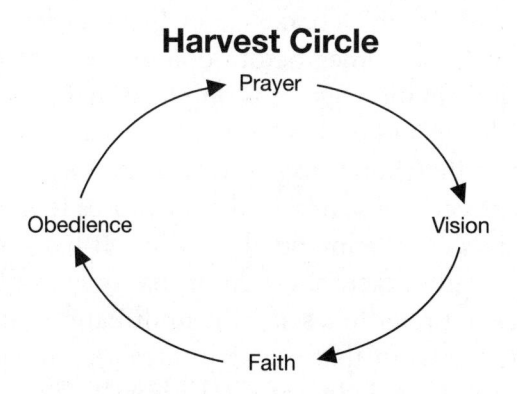

Prayer → Vision → Faith → Obedience → (Prayer)

Figure 5. Harvest Circle.

LEADERSHIP FOR THE TASK

God is preparing many local congregations for a time of unparalleled blessing in mission and ministry. As they develop and adopt a "harvest theology," God will open the doors of opportunity for effective outreach. The promise of God is that he will also provide the necessary leadership for this endeavor. "Then will I give you shepherds after my own heart, who will lead you with knowledge and understanding" (Jeremiah 3:15).

That is a powerful promise for the church! Be sure to translate "shepherds" with the word "leaders." The prophet, in the context of the scripture, is calling Judah to repentance during the time of Josiah, the reformer. If the nation will respond faithfully to God, then the promise is that God will raise up leaders "after my own heart" who will lead with knowledge and understanding.

Perhaps the most crucial quality of leadership for the church is found in this verse. To be a person "after the heart of God" is the foundation of leadership. All leadership, and followership for that matter, must begin with this simple fact. We must be people after the heart of God!

The quality of our relationship with God is the keystone upon which leadership is built. That union with God is a prerequisite, an unconditional requirement, if we are to engage in ministry which honors God. Being a friend of God, a servant of God, comes before doing the work of God.

In the information age, it is only reasonable to assume that "knowledge and understanding" are sorely needed for leadership in the church today. It doesn't take long, however, to discover in a search of the scriptures that acquired information is not the intended meaning. It has nothing to do with the glut of facts and figures that is so available today. It does not refer to a scientific information explosion.

Rather, the truth that the scriptures seek to convey is rooted in our knowledge of God himself. The wisdom literature of the Old Testament emphasizes this. "The fear of the Lord is the beginning of knowledge..." (Proverbs 1:7). "The fear of the Lord is the beginning of wisdom, and knowledge of the Holy One is understanding" (Proverbs 9:10).

Please recognize that this is not knowing "about" God in an intellectual sense. The knowledge of God comes, in the concept of the Old Testament, from a personal, intimate covenant of love and trust with him. This is a knowledge that flows out of a deep relationship of wonder for the redemptive nature of God and the response of obedience to him.

To lead with this revelation of God is the basis of our leadership. It is the "knowledge" upon which all other information that we use must be founded.

The word "understanding" expands this truth even further. It carries the meaning of having insight into God's intentions and purposes for humankind. "Understanding" is the discerning of the plan of God as it applies ultimately to the everyday life situation.

Leadership, then, which leads on the bedrock of "knowledge and understanding" is fundamentally a spiritual endeavor growing out of our relationship to God. It is guided by the leader's personal apprehension of who God is and what he is up to in the world. It is informed by the practical application of that "knowledge" in the affairs of human beings so that through obedience they may be in harmony with God and each other in accomplishing God's will.

This principle was certainly at work in the early church. When difficulty arose, the apostles instructed the church in Jerusalem to choose from their number those who were "known to be full of the Spirit and wisdom" (Acts 6:3). These men were then commissioned to leadership roles which enabled the church to function effectively. Their leadership was predicated on their spiritual readiness, their practical acumen and their relationships within the body of believers.

As I view the church and its ministry today, it is clear to me that the call of God is for leaders "after the heart of God who will lead with knowledge and understanding." All of the leadership skills and abilities that are needed proceed from this foundation.

PARTNERSHIP IN MISSION AND MINISTRY

I want to affirm that God is calling local congregations to a bold new thrust in their mission and ministry to the twenty-first century and beyond. We are to be "God's people on mission through ministry." He has given us the assurance that if the church will "anticipate the harvest" and follow the design of God for the church he will provide the leadership and the "know how."

It is evident to me that if we are to mobilize the church to be God's people on mission the local church must forge a new partnership to accomplish the task. This will mean that pastors, congregational leaders, state and national leaders must work together in harmony concentrating on our shared responsibility. As partners, we can take our place in the whole body of Christ so that it "grows and builds itself up in love, as each part does its work" (Ephesians 4:16).

Lay leaders, in this decade, are being asked to take a larger share of responsibility for the mission and ministry of the whole body of Christ. I would call upon each congregation to aggressively build on this trend as a source of strength and new vitality. Let us challenge our gifted leaders to assume their rightful place as partners in the mission and ministry of the church.

The challenge before the local congregation today is to be effective in its mission and ministry. To be spiritually alive and engaged in the Great Commission will demand our greatest effort even as we place our total dependence upon God. We do have the assurance that God will prepare the church for the harvest according to his divine plan. If the local congregation "sows to please the Spirit," the church will "from the Spirit reap" a bountiful harvest of "eternal life." "Let us not become weary in well doing, for at the proper time we will reap a harvest if we do not give up" (Galatians 6:8,9).

Let us pledge to follow the call of God to "be" his people, to have his mission as our purpose and "do" his ministry among people. If we are able to give our hearts and hands to this task, as his people we will one day hear the voice of God saying, "Well done, good and faithful servant! Come and share your master's happiness" (Matthew 25:23).

ENDNOTES

[134] C. Peter Wagner, unpublished seminar notes, (Pasadena, California: Fuller Theological Seminary, August 1991).

[135] Rick Blumenberg, THE PRAYER SUPPORT SYSTEM (Grand Rapids, Michigan: Sagamore Books, 1986), 15.

[136] David Watson, CALLED AND COMMITTED (Wheaton, Illinois: Harold Shaw Publishers, 1982), 176, 177.

SOURCES CONSULTED

Anderson, Leith. A CHURCH FOR THE 21ST CENTURY. Minneapolis, Minnesota: Bethany House Publishers, 1992.

_____. DYING FOR CHANGE. Minneapolis, Minnesota: Bethany House Publishers, 1990.

Bakke, Ray. THE URBAN CHRISTIAN. Downers Grove, Illinois: InterVarsity Press, 1987.

Barker, Joel Arthur. THE POWER OF VISION. Burnsville, Minnesota: Charthouse Learning Corporation, 1990. video cassette.

_____. FUTURE EDGE. New York: William Morrow and Co., 1992.

Barna, George. WITHOUT A VISION, THE PEOPLE PERISH. Glendale, California: Barna Research Group Limited, 1991.

Barnhart, Clarence, ed. AMERICAN COLLEGE DICTIONARY. New York: Harper and Brothers Publishers, 1953.

Bennis, Warren and Burt Nanus. LEADERS: THE STRATEGIES FOR TAKING CHARGE. New York: Harper and Row, Publishers, 1985.

Blanchard, Ken. MANAGING THE JOURNEY: UNDERSTANDING AND IMPLEMENTING CHANGE. Schaumberg, Illinois: Video Publishing House, 1989. video cassette.

Blumenberg, Rick. THE PRAYER SUPPORT SYSTEM. Grand Rapids, Michigan: Sagamore Books, 1986.

Bugbee, Bruce L. NETWORKING: EQUIPPING THOSE WHO ARE SEEKING TO SEEKING TO SERVE. Pasadena, California: The Charles E. Fuller Institute, 1989, audio cassette.

Conn, Harvie M., ed. THEOLOGICAL PERSPECTIVE ON CHURCH GROWTH. Phillipsburg, New Jersey: Presbyterian and Reformed Publishing Co., 1976.

_____. A CLARIFIED VISION FOR URBAN MISSION. Grand Rapids, Michigan: Zondervan Publishing House, 1987.

Dale, Robert D. KEEPING THE DREAM ALIVE. Nashville, Tennessee: Broadman Press, 1988.

_____. TO DREAM AGAIN. Nashville, Tennessee: Broadman Press, 1981.

Dayton, Edward R. and Ted W. Engstrom. STRATEGY FOR LEADERSHIP. Old Tappan, New Jersey: Fleming H. Revell Co., 1979.

DISCOVER YOUR GIFTS. Grand Rapids, Michigan: Church Development Resources, 1983.

Drucker, Peter F. MANAGING THE NONPROFIT ORGANIZATION. New York: Harper Collins Publishers, 1990.

Dethmer, Jim. PASTORS' UPDATE MONTHLY CASSETTE PROGRAM. Pasadena, California: Charles E. Fuller Institute of Evangelism and Church Growth, September 1990.

Ellis, Joe S. THE CHURCH ON PURPOSE. Cincinnati, Ohio: Standard Publishing, 1982.

Engstrom, Ted W. THE MAKING OF A CHRISTIAN LEADER. Grand Rapids, Michigan: Zondervan Publishing House, 1976.

_____. A TIME FOR COMMITMENT. Grand Rapids, Michigan: Zondervan Publishing House, 1987.

Finney, John. UNDERSTANDING LEADERSHIP. London: Daybreak, 1989.

_____. unpublished seminar notes. Pasadena, California: Fuller Theological Seminary, January 1992.

Galloway, Dale E. 20/20 VISION. Portland, Oregon: Scott Publishing Company, 1986.

George, Carl F. HOW TO HANDLE CONFLICT AND CHANGE. Pasadena, California: Charles E. Fuller Institute of Evangelism and Church Growth, 1991, seminar on audio cassette.

_____. PREPARE YOUR CHURCH FOR THE FUTURE. Tarrytown, New York: Fleming H. Revell Co., 1991.

_____. unpublished seminar notes. Pasadena, California: Fuller Theological Seminary, August 1986.

George, Carl F. and Robert E. Logan. LEADING AND MANAGING YOUR CHURCH. Old Tappan, New Jersey: Fleming H. Revell Co. 1987.

Gibbs, Eddie. I BELIEVE IN CHURCH GROWTH. Grand Rapids, Michigan: William B. Eerdmans Publishing Company, 1981.

_____. FOLLOWED OR PUSHED?. London: MARC Europe, British Church Growth Association, 1987.

Haugk, Kenneth C. ANTAGONISTS IN THE CHURCH. Minneapolis, Minnesota: Augsburg Publishing House, 1988.

Hetrick, Gale. LAUGHTER AMONG THE TRUMPETS. Lansing, Michigan: The Church of God in Michigan, 1980.

Hunter, George. G., III. TO SPREAD THE POWER. Nashville: Abingdon Press, 1987.

_____. YOUR CHURCH HAS PERSONALITY. Nashville: Abingdon Press, 1985.

Huttenlocker, Keith. CONFLICT AND CARING. Grand Rapids, Michigan: Zondervan Publishing House, 1988.

LAY MOBILIZATION MANUAL. Pasadena, California: Charles E. Fuller Institute of Evangelism and Church Growth, 1988.

Leas, Speed B. LEADERSHIP AND CONFLICT. Nashville: Abingdon Press, 1982.

Lewis, G. Douglass. RESOLVING CHURCH CONFLICTS. San Francisco: Harper and Row, Publishers, 1981.

Lindgren, Alvin J. and Norman Shawchuck. LET MY PEOPLE GO. Nashville: Abingdon Press, 1980.

Logan, Robert E. BEYOND CHURCH GROWTH. Old Tappan, New Jersey: Fleming H. Revell Co., 1989.

Lowe, Conrad. PASTORS' UPDATE MONTHLY CASSETTE PROGRAM. Vol. 3, No. 10. Pasadena, California: Charles E. Fuller Institute of Evangelism and Church Growth, July 1992.

Malphurs, Aubrey. DEVELOPING A VISION FOR MINISTRY IN THE 21ST CENTURY. Grand Rapids, Michigan: Baker Book House, 1992.

Maxwell, John E. LAY MINISTRY. Spring Valley, California: Injoy, 1989, seminar on video cassette.

McGavran, Donald and George G. Hunter, III. CHURCH GROWTH: STRATEGIES THAT WORK. Nashville: Abingdon, 1980.

Miller, Herb. THE VITAL CONGREGATION. Nashville: Abingdon Press, 1990.

Mylander, Charles. SECRETS FOR GROWING CHURCHES. San Francisco: Harper and Row, Publishers, 1979.

Nuechterlein, Anne Marie. IMPROVING YOUR MULTIPLE STAFF MINISTRY. Minneapolis, Minnesota: Augsburg Fortress, 1989.

Peters, George W. A THEOLOGY OF CHURCH GROWTH. Grand Rapids, Michigan: Zondervan Publishing House, 1981.

Schaller, Lyle E. GETTING THINGS DONE. Nashville: Abingdon Press, 1986.

_____. GROWING PLANS. Nashville: Abingdon Press, 1983.

_____. LOOKING IN THE MIRROR. Nashville: Abingdon Press, 1984.

_____. THE SMALL CHURCH IS DIFFERENT. Nashville: Abingdon Press. 1982.

_____. THE MULTIPLE STAFF AND THE LARGER CHURCH. Nashville: Abingdon Press, 1985.

_____. THE PASTOR AND THE PEOPLE, Revised. Nashville: Abingdon Press, 1986.

Shawchuck, Norman. HOW TO MANAGE CONFLICT IN THE CHURCH, Vol. 1. Indianapolis, Indiana: Spiritual Growth Resources, 1983.

Smalley, Gary and John Trent. THE BLESSING. Nashville: Thomas Nelson Publishers, 1986.

Snyder, Howard A. THE COMMUNITY OF THE KING. Downers Grove, Illinois: Inter-Varsity Press, 1977.

_____. LIBERATING THE CHURCH. Downers Grove, Illinois: Inter-Varsity Press, 1983.

_____. THE PROBLEM OF WINE SKINS. Downers Grove, Illinois: Inter-Varsity Press, 1975.

Stanley, Paul D. and J. Robert Clinton. CONNECTING. Colorado Springs, Colorado: NavPress, 1992.

Tillapaugh, Frank R. UNLEASHING THE CHURCH. Ventura, California: Regal Books, 1982.

Van Engen, Charles. THE GROWTH OF THE TRUE CHURCH. Amsterdam: Rodopi, 1981.

Wagner, C. Peter. CHURCH GROWTH AND THE WHOLE GOSPEL. San Francisco, California: Harper and Row, Publishers, 1981.

_____. LEADING YOUR CHURCH TO GROWTH. Ventura, California: Regal Books, 1984

_____. unpublished seminar notes. Pasadena, California: Fuller Theological Seminary, August 1986.

_____. unpublished seminar notes. Pasadena, California: Fuller Theological Seminary, August 1991.

_____. YOUR CHURCH CAN BE HEALTHY. Nashville: Abingdon Press, 1979.

_____. YOUR SPIRITUAL GIFTS CAN HELP YOUR CHURCH GROW. Ventura, California: Regal Books, 1979.

Watson, David. CALLED AND COMMITTED. Wheaton, Illinois: Harold Shaw Publishers, 1982.

_____. I BELIEVE IN EVANGELISM. Grand Rapids, Michigan: William B. Eerdmans Publishing Company, 1976.

Withrow, Oral. OUR CHURCH CAN GROW. Anderson, Indiana: Warner Press, 1991.

Wright, G. Ernest. GOD WHO ACTS: BIBLICAL THEOLOGY AS RECITAL. London: S C M Press LTD, 1952.

Yankelovich, Daniel. "How Public Opinion Really Works." FORTUNE, 5 October 1992, 102 - 108.

Zunkel, C. Wayne. CHURCH GROWTH UNDER FIRE. Scottdale, Pennsylvania: Herald Press, 1987.